FOCUS ON EDUCATION
Series Editor: Trevor Kerry

Teaching English
A teaching skills workbook

Peter King
B.A., M.A., M.Ed.
Senior Lecturer in Education
Loughborough University

Macmillan Education

© Peter King 1985

All rights reserved. No reproduction, copy or transmission of this publication may be made without written permission.

No paragraph of this publication may be reproduced, copied or transmitted save with written permission or in accordance with the provisions of the Copyright Act 1956 (as amended).

Any person who does any unauthorised act in relation to this publication may be liable to criminal prosecution and civil claims for damages.

First published 1985
Reprinted 1986

Published by
MACMILLAN EDUCATION LTD
Houndmills, Basingstoke, Hampshire RG21 2XS
and London
Companies and representatives
throughout the world

Printed in Hong Kong

ISBN 0-333-37641-2

ACKNOWLEDGEMENTS

The author and publishers wish to thank the following who have kindly given permission for the use of copyright material:

Rex Collings Ltd for the poem 'Telephone Conversation' by Wole Soyinka; Croom Helm Ltd for an extract from *Teaching English* (1982) by T. Evans; Faber and Faber Ltd for the poem 'Wind' from *The Hawk in the Rain* by Ted Hughes; Hodder & Stoughton Ltd for an extract from *The Incredible Journey* by Sheila Burnford; Oxford University Press for an extract from *Every English Teacher* (1974) by Anthony Adams and John Pearce; Ward Lock Educational Co. Ltd for an extract from *Thinking About English* (1979) by Michael Paffard.

CONTENTS

Editor's Preface 4
Introduction 5

PART 1 PREPARING TO TEACH ENGLISH

Topic 1   What is English?   6
Topic 2   Activities in English   10
Topic 3   Lesson-planning   15
Topic 4   Classroom organisation   23

PART 2 TEACHING ENGLISH

Focus 1   What's in a question?   33
Focus 2   Handling class discussions   37
Focus 3   Talk in small groups   39
Focus 4   Ways into a class novel   41
Focus 5   Looking at poems   44
Focus 6   Reading in bottom gear   47
Focus 7   Planning for writing   49
Focus 8   Structuring writing tasks   52
Focus 9   Responding to writing   55

PART 3 REFLECTIONS ON EXPERIENCE

Topic A   Review of teaching   59
Topic B   Keeping records   61
Topic C   What is grammar?   63
Topic D   Creative writing   64
Topic E   Fiction for teenagers   66
Topic F   The mass media   69

Selected reading   72

EDITOR'S PREFACE

The titles in this series are designed to examine basic teaching skills in their respective subject areas. Each title is laid out as a workbook so that the practitioner can utilise his or her own classroom as a basis for progressive professional self-development.

Impetus for the series came out of the DES-financed Teacher Education Project, which ran from 1976 to 1980 in the Universities of Nottingham, Leicester and Exeter. That project explored general teaching skills: class management, questioning, explaining, and the handling of mixed ability classes and exceptional pupils. A direct outcome from the work of the Teacher Education Project was a series of skills workbooks under the general title *Focus*, which was published by Macmillan during the years 1981 and 1982.

It is, perhaps, a measure of the success of the *Focus* series that I was approached by a number of colleagues in the involved universities with the proposal for a 'curriculum' series of workbooks which would apply some of the teaching skills highlighted and researched by the project to specific subject areas.

Each title in the current curriculum series is aimed at subject teachers in the appropriate field. Our corporate intention is to make each workbook immediately relevant to the needs of three main groups of users: qualified teachers of the subject in question; teachers qualified in some other discipline who find themselves pressed into service on less familiar ground; and students in training in the subject area concerned. Past experience has led us to believe that each exercise is adaptable for use at various levels of sophistication according to the stage reached by the user and to his or her own needs.

Each workbook has a tripartite format. Part 1 is intended to start the user thinking about issues in the particular curriculum area, and the activities designed for this purpose can often be carried out away from the classroom itself. In Part 2 a collection of practical exercises encourages teachers to become more self-aware and to scrutinise their own practice. Part 3 helps the teachers reflect on practice and experience by relating classroom events to research and theory. Within this basic structure individual authors are given some flexibility to interpret their own theme.

The series makes frequent demands on teachers to get together in order to watch one another at work: a process we have labelled 'observational pairing'. Traditionally the classroom has been 'a fine and private place' as Marvell might have put it. We believe that professional self-respect demands that a more open attitude should prevail.

It is especially opportune to be producing the curriculum series of workbooks at a time when economic stringencies are making in-roads into the education service in general and into in-service provision in particular. There is mounting public pressure for increased accountability by the teaching profession. This series will, we believe, help to make teachers more analytical in their teaching and more articulate in expressing the rationale for their work. It will also fill a void for really practical advice for all those whose jobs involve a responsibility for professional training, as university and college tutors, inspectors, advisers, teachers' centre wardens, headteachers, and heads of subject departments.

Dr Trevor Kerry
*Doncaster Metropolitan Institute
of Higher Education*

INTRODUCTION

English is not a subject with a clear-cut body of knowledge, nor a universally accepted methodology. This is not necessarily something to lament. A fixed content and uniform approach are more likely to lead to unreflective, narrow and rigid teaching, a condition unlikely to promote genuine desire to develop true understanding in the learner. Being unable to slot into a preconceived view of what he is to do, the new English teacher must learn to see the diversity of his subject as a possibility for personal reflection and experimentation within alternative approaches.

This book does not discuss the diversities and alternatives. It encourages teachers to make an active exploration of a range of key skills required of them if they are to be reflective about their practices. It introduces the first steps in coming to terms with those skills and their attendant attitudes by looking, briefly, at the different models of the subject currently in evidence in our classrooms. It moves on to see how the wide range of aims can be transformed into practical classroom procedures. It is argued that this can be done by seeing English as providing pupils with experience and practice in all the language modes. The role of the teacher is to offer learning experiences in each mode, through which the pupil is guided and supported in a journey of growth, not just in language development, but in the development of a sense of identity and awareness of self and the surrounding world. The major part of the book suggests practical activities for the reader to undertake in his or her classroom in order to begin the continuous process of becoming a professional who is as much a learner as those in his charge.

If this approach centres on the skills demanded of both teacher and learner, it is important to stress at the outset that this is not the same as saying English is *just* a skills-based subject or that teaching is a matter of skills acquisition. Skills are the practical embodiment of beliefs, attitudes, relationships and values. Such skills as are here described are the direct consequence of adopting the procedural principles mentioned in the first topic of the book, and these are but the expression of the *relationship* between the English teachers and their pupils as co-users of language as the most expressive and communicative of the human arts.

Peter King
University of Loughborough

Part 1 PREPARING TO TEACH ENGLISH

**Topic 1
WHAT IS ENGLISH?**

A group of teachers of various subjects (history, maths, chemistry and geography) were discussing with an English teacher the similarities and differences between their subjects and English. Some of the features of their subjects which were mentioned are listed below.

**Activity 1:
Comparing English &
other subjects**

Place a tick in the appropriate column to indicate which features you think occur in English and which in the other subjects.

Features: the subject . . .	English	Others
. . . has a body of knowledge to be passed on (facts, principles, laws)		
. . . is mastered in a series of incremental steps proceeding in a strict order		
. . . is centrally concerned with personal and social development		
. . . is as much concerned with affective as with cognitive development		
. . . requires progressive mastery of distinct concepts and specialist vocabulary		
. . . passes on a tradition of cultural heritage		

Obviously the distinctions between English and the other subjects do not mean there are no similarities, but they do point to the particular attributes of English as a school subject. Michael Paffard illuminates the nature of the subject in *Thinking About English* (Ward Lock Educational, 1979):

English is paradoxically both less and more than a subject. It is less than a subject in the sense that it is not primarily concerned to teach *about* language or literature or anything else. There is little in the way of an agreed body of information which has to be transmitted from teacher to learner and this is what makes many school English syllabuses such phoney documents. Old fashioned ones . . . unashamedly made out of formal grammar and the history of literature such a corpus of knowledge that could be taught and tested. . . . But English is mainly concerned with doing rather than knowing, in a word, with skills and more particularly with skills of expression, communication, discovery and evaluation. . . . It is concerned with personal growth and with our cultural heritage. It deals with levels of personal experience and the matrix of language from which all other specialist concerns develop. What makes it more than a subject then, is tied up with the nature of language, the immense complexity and variety of the purposes for which we use it, and the nature of literature, the immense variety and complexity of the human experience it can convey.

English is not so much a body of knowledge as a complex of skills: talking, reading, writing, listening and skills of expression and communication. However, the learning of English is not simply a matter of acquiring skills: The focus of English is the *use* of those skills in the service of individual pupils' growth in self-awareness, understanding of those around them, imagination, sympathy, creativity, thought and feeling. English is the *process* of engaging in language activities and not the product of assimilating knowledge. In English 'we see not only the intellectual organising of experience that goes on in many other subjects, but also a parallel ordering of the feelings and attitudes with which pupils encounter life around them.' (John Dixon, 1975). It's easier to understand the contribution of English to the education of the emotions if we remind ourselves of the unique effects the possession of language bestows on us.

The scope of language

Animals' communication systems are instinctual and limited compared with verbal communication in humans where language is learned and capable of complex development. Most animals are restricted to signalling the equivalent of 'Get off my patch!' or 'It's the mating season, whoopee!' whereas human speech and writing create scope for a greater degree of cooperation and a greater command over self, others and the surrounding world.

Language is an essential human tool for representing the world permitting (a) conceptualisation – ordering and patterning experience to make it 'thinkable', (b) the expression of abstract ideas – allowing hypothetical-deductive thought and freeing people from the immediate present and the concrete particular, (c) the growth of knowledge and its transmission over time and space – accelerating understanding.

In this way, the possession of language may be said to give people the power of making meaning. Words throw a network of order over reality allowing people to frame their experience and express and communicate their identity at the same time as they 'create' what there is to be so expressed and communicated.

Learning to use our language is the process of meaning-making, of understanding ideas, feelings and attitudes, making it possible for us to be learning, creating and communicating beings. And we learn language by using it: the amount, variety and quality of the words uttered in our presence being the essential experience contributing to the level of our mastery. Language is intimately connected with our growth of identity as a person: with our sense of ourself, with our understanding and reciprocal relationships with others, with our feelings, fantasies, dreams, frustrations, ideas, hopes, memories, with the whole living tissue of our encounters with life.

Language is me	Language is imagining, designing, creating, destroying
Language is you	
Language is people	Language is control and persuasion
Language is what people do	Language is communication
Language is loving and hurting	Language is laughter
Language is clothes, faces, gestures, responses	Language is growth

Language is me
'The limits of my language are the limits of my world'

So, the first answer to 'What is English?' is:

it is the process and practice of all those activities we engage in through language.

The focus for English as a subject is language in all its variety of forms and functions (from the language of conversation, anecdote and jokes to the condensed energy of the language of poetry). It is concerned with the modes and skills of TALKING, WRITING, READING and LISTENING. The broad aim of English teaching is to intervene in a naturally developing process to enhance, accelerate and enliven the mastery of each of these modes. It's not teaching *about* language but practising its use.

**Activity 2:
Examining some aims of English teaching**

What kinds of goals do you think the English teacher should aim for in the light of this acknowledgement of the power and purpose of language? Try to list what you consider to be the important aims.

When a group of experienced English teachers was asked to carry out this activity, they agreed eventually to this list of aims:

> To develop basic skills in talking, reading and writing so that pupils may express and communicate in a variety of situations for a variety of purposes and a variety of audiences.
>
> To encourage reading as a pleasurable, rewarding and useful activity.
>
> To develop the ability to read a wide range of texts with understanding.
>
> To increase confidence in handling written language and to display the capacity to choose styles appropriate to the form, function and audience.
>
> To provoke a care for, and appreciation of, precision in handling language.
>
> To introduce a sample of the best literature in such a way that pupils desire to explore it further for themselves.
>
> To encourage a disciplined and sensitive attention to language in all forms so that the individual may learn to discriminate the good from the meretricious, the informative from the persuasive, the honest from the sentimental, the live from the dead, the creative from the cliché.
>
> To cultivate the power to imagine, to feel a way into experiences other than one's own, as well as to describe and evaluate one's own.
>
> To develop the capacity to sustain and communicate an abstract argument and illustrate it concretely in both writing and talking.
>
> To help the emergence of an individual capacity to form values, attitudes and meanings that help pupils to understand themselves and others better.

These (and additional aims) can be expressed in many ways. It is the English teacher's responsibility to try and achieve them within the limits set by his or her pupils' age and ability. It is done through attention to all the language modes: talking, reading, writing, drama, and, in particular, through the use of literature. The important point to note here is that English includes, but goes far beyond, the concept of basic skills. English is involved with the pupils' imagination and feelings as well. Language and literature are used to explore our pupils' sense of identity and their affective response to the world.

Stated like this, however, there appears to be a clearer consensus over aims than actually exists. The priorities within such a list of aims can be variously interpreted by different teachers and departments. As a result, there are tensions within the subject. Perhaps the best way of expressing these tensions is to set out the assumptions that lie behind teachers' adoptions of aims by sketching the 'models' of English currently affecting the subject. Below is a brief sketch of four models adapted from *Teaching English Across the Ability Range*, R.W. Mills (Ward Lock, 1977).

Activity 3:
Examining some models of English teaching

For each of the following models try to state briefly what aspects of the aims of English might be in danger of being under-rated.

> *Basic skills*: Primarily concerned with functional literacy, stressing minimum competence in all pupils to cope with daily language demands. Language is focus; literature for most able.
>
> *Cultural heritage*: All pupils to be introduced to examples of good literature as a humanising influence and example of understanding of personal and social values.

Sociological stance: Use of language and literature to explore issues and themes relevant to present day and to help individual pupil relate to larger social context.

Personal growth: Individual learner, with needs, beliefs, and experiences, brought into relation to all language modes, including literature. Focus on ways words organise our perception of life in order to promote awareness, articulacy, and affective development.

balance is the key word.

These are necessarily simplified versions of the different approaches to English. No single teacher will necessarily operate under just one approach, but his or her choice of aims will reflect a bias towards one or two of the models. All the models have strengths and weaknesses but to achieve the necessary balance it is perhaps the last model which can most readily assimilate the insights of the others.

Thus, a further answer to 'What is English?' is:
> *it teaches not only how to communicate effectively (literacy skills), but also self-expression and the means whereby language may interpret our personal and social lives (developing individual potential).*

These aims and models lead to certain interpretations of the English teacher's role and these principles apply to the way in which his or her teaching is approached.

Procedural principles

The teacher is responsible for . . .

... the provision of the widest possible range of situations for using all modes of language;
... working outwards from pupils' language capacities and making use of their experiences, ideas, feelings, attitudes;
... responding to pupils' individual differences;
... making language-work as realistic as possible as language is developed by putting it to work, not by doing 'dummy runs' or isolated exercises;
... creating an atmosphere in which pupils trust the teacher to respect their ideas, feelings and attitudes;
... providing constant opportunities for pupils to talk and explore ideas;
... active encouragement and support of pupils, looking more for things to reward than penalise so that even the least able have a taste of success;
... use of 'third ground': that is stories, plays, poems, on which pupils and teacher meet to explore their experience;
... acting as stimulator of ideas, provider of resources, guide to learning, and promoter of active pupil participation rather than authoritarian scourge;
... doing and showing how, rather than passive receiving and telling about.

These principles provide guidance to the way our aims should be realised in classroom activities. They demand certain skills from the teacher and the remainder of this book will help you to reflect upon these aims and try out these activities and skills in the classroom.

For further study

1 Obtain a copy of your school's English syllabus or statement of policy. Read it alongside the aims, models and procedural principles outlined here. What assumptions about the nature of English are implied by the syllabus?
2 Perhaps the most interesting argument for a personal growth model of English is in *Growth Through English*, J. Dixon (Oxford rev. ed. 1975).
3 If you are interested in the changing competing claims on English, read M. Mathieson, *The Preachers of Culture* (Allen & Unwin, 1975) or D. Allen, *English Teaching since 1965* (Heinemann Educational, 1979).

Topic 2 ACTIVITIES IN ENGLISH

Section A Developing objectives

We saw in Topic 1 that English has many aims and that there are various approaches to teaching the subject which reflect underlying tensions between differing priorities among teachers. We have also seen that those tensions may be held in balance if we adopt an approach that is concerned with our pupils' overall language development and the contribution that makes to the individual's personal, emotional and social growth. In *Every English Teacher* (Oxford, 1974) Adams and Pearce describe this approach:

> The central tasks of English are to foster the personal growth of children and to increase their capacity to use language for all those purposes which their lives make necessary.
> If we had to give this view a catch-phrase label, we would call it a 'competence and identity' model. We think it peculiarly important to see the two components of this model, not as distinct and separate identities, but as inter-penetrating elements: an adolescent whose competence with language is supremely gifted may so lack a sense of his own identity or a sensitive awareness of people as to be able to use his language skills only for destructive ends. In the same way, a child of 12 who is mature and sensitive beyond his years will be unable to turn these virtues to any account if he is seriously deficient in selecting what to say to people and how to say it.

The label we choose to describe our subject is immaterial. What matters is what we do in our lessons. Our clue to what the activities of the English classroom should be lies in Adams and Pearce's insistence on the inter-weaving of the practice and mastery of skills with a sensitivity towards the individual learner's sense of himself or herself and his or her world.

Pupils learn from the activities in which they engage. These activities of talking, reading and writing are the processes of language which the pupils master by doing, not by being told. The content of a lesson may be anything through which these processes can be initiated and which can interest the children. A lesson's theme or subject can come from almost anywhere. On the one hand, it might arise from reading a class novel and associated talk and writing that helps pupils to penetrate the experience of the narrative (a pre-planned series of lessons) and, on the other hand, the content of a lesson might arise quite unexpectedly as the teacher grasps something emerging spontaneously from the pupils' interests.

For instance, a teacher entering the class overheard a vociferous argument about a local football match and its accompanying 'trouble' on the terraces. He decided to abandon his lesson plan to conduct a lesson which took up this talk and channelled it into a discussion about football hooliganism. This led to writing on the subject in the style of a newspaper feature article.

What unites these two approaches is not their content but their concern to create language opportunities.

This next activity will help you to consolidate your grasp of these aims and start you thinking about how to actualise them in your classroom.

**Activity 4:
Looking at aims in practice**

There follow brief descriptions of four different lessons (or parts of lessons) representing different language modes as their prime focus. Read the descriptions; then review the aims and procedural principles listed in Topic 1. For each lesson, *note what you think the teacher's aims were, the skills the pupils are practising* (try to say more than 'reading' or 'writing') and *what they might have learned* in terms of the 'competence and identity' model.

Activity

The class had been reading an extract from an autobiography about children who 'got up to mischief', were caught and punished. They talked about the motives of the children, the attitudes of the grown-ups and whether the children should have been punished. In small groups they swapped experiences of their own of being caught doing something wrong. This led to personal writing on the theme, with the teacher stressing the need to express the feelings of both the children and the grown-ups involved.
(2nd year)

A simulation of a public enquiry into the siting of a 'pop' festival. The teacher is a neutral chairperson organising the enquiry. Twelve pupils are divided into two sides with one side supporting the venture and the other opposed. Each pupil plays the role of a character (e.g. festival organiser or local shopkeeper) and has pointers to the sort of person he or she is and the stance to take from a 'character card'. His or her speech and the ensuing questioning of each side are left to him or her. Other pupils question the two sides. Finally a vote is taken, the chairman sums up, and then the whole class discusses the proceedings.
(4th year)

Silent, private reading of books of the pupils' own choice. The room has books everywhere and the walls are covered in posters and pupils' work. The pupils are allowed to exchange books. All types of book are available and the pupils enter what they read in a diary. The teacher goes round quietly chatting at some length to individuals, talking about their books. Later the teacher and several pupils read extracts from some books, saying why others might like to look at them.
(1st year)

Comment

The class has just read *Adolf* by D.H. Lawrence, a story of a wild rabbit brought home by the father but later released because it could not be tamed. Pupils work in pairs from a worksheet which has several different questions and activities to help them think about the story and about their own experiences with family pets. After half an hour, they report their joint answers to the rest of the class, and the teacher develops their points and encourages discussion.
(3rd year)

Section B Planning for language development
Part of the role of English in the curriculum is to intervene in children's growth of language competencies in order to shape and expand that natural development. If this is so, it is useful for the English teacher to consider what kinds of language experiences might be provided at which stages of a pupil's school career.

Unfortunately it is not possible to make a precise list of the levels of linguistic competence that a pupil might be expected to have reached by a particular age. Individual development is too variable. Nor is it helpful to spell out the attainment level of technical language skills at different ages, for example, syntactical development, or vocabulary acquisition. What can be done, and is more useful to the teacher, is to ask what kinds of experiences in reading, writing, and talking/listening are appropriate for pupils to undergo at particular ages if they are to achieve the aims discussed in Topic 1. As we discovered there, the task of the English teacher is to provide his or her pupils with opportunities to experience and make use of the widest possible range of language functions by making a conscious attempt to enhance and refine the pupils' natural language acquisition. Beginning with what the pupils already know about and can do with the spoken and written word, the English teacher must provide activities and learning experiences which will lead them into richer and more resourceful uses of their language.

English exploits the pupil's opinions and experiences through constructive discussion; it broadens these opinions and experiences through a wide range of literature. It encourages the pupil's initiative to stimulate written work and uses spelling, punctuation and grammar rules in the pupil's interests, waiving them where quality and quantity rather than undistinguished accuracy are the priorities. It is about planning and pruning and experimenting with ideas and approaches.

T. Evans, Teaching English (Croom Helm, 1982)

Pupils must receive a balance of reading, writing and talking activities with goals in each language mode appropriate to their age. Language development does not have the clear-cut incremental progress that is alleged to occur in acquiring mathematical knowledge, and it therefore contains much repetition of the various language skills. The English syllabus is more of a spiral curriculum, continually taking up the same skills at an increasingly higher, more complex and subtle level of thought, feeling and expression.

The following activity builds on this idea of a spiral development. Its purpose is to help you construct a guiding framework for matching classroom learning activities with the goals of language competence at various ages from 11 to 16. This is a crucial step in considering aims and planning a syllabus.

	YEAR 1	YEAR 2	YEAR 3	YEAR 4/5
READING	**A1** – widening interest in fiction, catching curiosity, encouraging active response – as stimulus to personal talk/writing – comprehension (varied tests): attention to ideas, effect of word choice, expression of mood, atmosphere ('the way words work') – poetry: emphasis on sound/rhythm	**A2** – fiction/stories allowing personal identification – looking at characters and relationships – widening experience of poetry (narrative, ballad, lyric): emphasis on structure – comprehension: including following arguments, explanations and instructions	**A3** – fiction supplemented by factual texts – looking at creation of mood/atmosphere/feeling – poetry: features of poetic style (figurative language/imagery, etc.) – comprehension: beyond literal meaning to interpretative understanding	**A4/5** – stories/poems looking at life from other people's viewpoints – wider choice of genres (including biography/travel/essays) – comprehension: evaluating writer's bias/arguments/opinions – sharpening critical consciousness (theme/style)
WRITING	**B1** – stories arising from reading – descriptive writing based on close observation/emphasising senses – play with words (games of sound/word pattern) introducing creative patterning/sense of form – simple poetic forms (emphasis on imagery/rhythm)	**B2** – narrative supplemented by personal anecdote/experience – simple reports/accounts of 'what happened' – how to order ideas/explanations – greater stress on writing about people (feelings in real or imagined situation)	**B3** – expressive/exploratory writing utilising interest in relationships with others – recording/reporting events or experiences – widening non-fictional modes (instructions, letters, discursive forms)	**B4/5** – full range of argumentative/discursive/persuasive/informative modes and exploration of social issues – summarising arguments – beginnings of evaluative/critical writing
TALKING	**C1** – personal anecdotes (own experiences/family/friends) – sharing personal experiences in small group talk – talk arising from reading and leading into writing – talk games to build confidence	**C2** – talk in pairs/small groups round reading/writing/activities (including prediction/sequencing/oral comprehension) – simple group role-play	**C3** – supporting/opposing points of view in small groups (beginning to stand back from personal opinion and consider evidence) – class discussion round topics emerging from reading – improvised drama exploring different perspectives on familiar situations	**C4/5** – small group work on problems/issues of social kind – prepared talks and improving formal speaking to audience – enquiries/debates – role-play including mock interviews

Activity 5:
Matching learning activities to aims

With one or more colleagues read carefully the framework of aims on page 13. Then take a pile of index cards and mark each one with the number of one of the boxes from the framework (1A, 1B, 1C, 2A, 2B, etc.).

1 Each member of the group in turn is to write on each of the cards ONE suggestion for a classroom activity that would be appropriate as a means of advancing towards one of the aims indicated on the framework for that particular age, e.g. *A2, looking at characters/relationships in a novel.*
Suggested activity:
pupils in small groups looking at different incidents in the novel to decide what they tell us about the characters.

2 When each person has completed their suggestion for all the cards, go through them as a group and decide how each activity will accomplish those aims. At the end of this exercise each group member will possess the beginnings of a syllabus for the 11-16 age range.

Please note

(a) Basic skills (grammar, punctuation, spelling) are not included on the framework. It is assumed that attention to such skills will be paid at every stage of a syllabus whenever the work of the pupils reveals the need for corrective exercises.
(b) At each stage the aims of the earlier stages are carried forward. It should not be assumed, for instance, that the early aim when reading novels of concentrating on characters and their relationships would not be included in working on a novel in fourth and fifth years.

For further study

1 Obtain an example of an English Department syllabus. Go through the aims for each year indicated in that syllabus and list the kinds of activities you think suitable for achieving those aims.

2 You will find a very interesting but slightly different kind of framework of language development in David Jackson, *Continuity in Secondary English* (Methuen, 1983). A third example of language development with a discussion of how to employ a thematic approach (for an explanation of theme teaching, see Part 3, Topic A) is to be found in L.E.W. Smith, *Towards a New English Curriculum* (Dent, 1972).

**Topic 3
LESSON-PLANNING**

NOTE   To get the most from this topic you should discuss your ideas with an experienced teacher or tutor.

Effective lessons rarely just happen. Even when the occasional unexpected success occurs spontaneously it is most likely to happen to the teacher who has had sufficient experience to allow him to recognise the productive incident from among a dozen events which, if followed, would lead nowhere. Spontaneous success favours a prepared mind, and it is indispensable for the less experienced teacher to exercise forethought. That means planning lessons ahead of teaching them.

The act of planning gives us a sense of direction, of goals, and the opportunity to reflect upon our choice of strategies for achieving these goals. It also permits us to be clearer about the criteria for assessing pupils' response. It makes the efficient organisation of resources more possible and it helps create continuity and coherence between separate lessons. A well-intentioned muddle will not do and we cannot wait, Micawber-like, for something to turn up to inspire us during the lesson itself. But planning need not prevent flexibility or spoil spontaneity. Indeed good planning allows for the possibility of the unforeseen digression that quickly reveals itself to be an unexpectedly rich avenue of exploration. Planning makes us focus on our goals and on what we hope our pupils will learn; and such an informed position helps us recognise more quickly the possible merit of a pupil's apparent digression. Nevertheless, no plan should become a Procrustean bed preventing any deviations or alterations.

Bearing this in mind, regard the lesson outlines that you read in this section as *guidelines and not blueprints*. Activities 6-8 should give you some idea of (a) how to structure a lesson, varying activities and planning for pupil participation, (b) the different kinds of lessons and the essentials of good planning, (c) the importance of defining aims in practical terms.

**Activity 6:
Planning for variety
and involvement**

A good lesson has VIBES: Variety
Interest
Blocks of activities
Engages with pupils' experience
Starts and ends clearly

Overleaf is an outline of a fairly typical English lesson which has these attributes. Alongside the description of what happened in the lesson you can read the reasons that the teacher gave for the shape and structure.

Note in particular how she took pains to have a *variety of activities and how she tried to involve the class and keep them active.*

After studying this outline, choose a topic to work on with one of your own classes. Plan a single lesson (which may lead to other lessons on the same topic), trying to give it VIBES and organising for active learning on the part of your pupils. When complete, your plan should show:

AIMS   your goal; what you want your pupils to learn or practise
CONTENT   choice of topic, resources, and ideas to be covered
METHOD   development of the lesson; your role and pupils' activities
OUTCOME   will it lead to writing, drama, reading or talk? connections with further lessons?

To help you assess the practicality and appropriateness of the plan, join with a colleague or tutor and together discuss why you made the decisions you did.

Example of a lesson

Class 4th year (average ability)   *Time* 1 hr 25 mins
Resources Kestrel For a Knave, Barry Hines (an extract). Copies for pupils.
Aims: (a) to explore and express a mood and emotion (anger)
(b) to emphasise how writing can be lively and vigorous through the selection of details in a description, and how feelings can be expressed in words so that someone else can see what emotions the writer is experiencing.

What happened	*Why teacher does it this way*
Teacher enters a rather noisy class. She looks very annoyed and turns to write on the blackboard without speaking. She then turns and glowers at the class and waits. She has written I AM ANGRY. The class subside and look uncertain, some even slightly guilty, waiting to see what she will do next.	IMPACT/STIMULUS attention-catching
After a pause and silence has descended she smiles broadly. The class looks relieved (they are not used to her being unpleasant with them!). She asks, 'What does it feel like when you are really very angry with someone?'	open question, inviting pupils' participation PERSONAL EXPERIENCE
She got some response but not a great deal and so had to ask more concrete questions like: 'When were you last angry with someone? Tell us about it? What happened?' She concentrated on asking, 'How would you describe what you felt inside yourself?' rather than on the details of the source of the anger.	GENUINE USE OF RESPONSE inviting exchange of personal anecdote concentrating on pupils' feelings
Response was much better and she wrote on the blackboard some of their descriptions of what they felt like. (17 mins)	confirming value of their own ideas
She introduces an extract from *Kestrel for a Knave* which describes a row between Billy and his mother. It is read twice, with short discussion about it in between. In the second reading a pupil takes the part of Billy and the teacher reads the mother's words. It is dramatically done.	TEXTUAL FOCUS contrasting activity on same theme underlines direction of lesson and provides variety
General talk on how the writer lets us know and feel what the boy and his mother feel.	close attention to text

She gets them in pairs to add several lines of description that give a more detailed account of their feelings. These are discussed and several suggestions are written on board. (20 mins)	PAIRS ACTIVITY widening experience of text providing model for later writing task
Introduction to a writing task. 'I want you to write about a time when you were angry. You have to let the reader really understand your feelings. Tell him how they could be seen in your face, your gestures, your actions and your words, and how the anger affected you inside. It can be a real incident like those you've mentioned, or you can imagine one. Probably it involves at least one other person.'	STRUCTURING WRITING TASK WRITING CLOSELY RELATED TO TALKING AND READING
She proceeds to start an example of her own on the board, in note form, paying particular attention to the need for lively details (e.g. fierce, blazing eyes, or 'I could have screamed with fury') and she gets some help and suggestions from the class.	careful instructions providing an example attention to language
She then points out the difference between annoyance and anger (something not clarified in their earlier examples), tells them how long they have and the minimum length that they can write. (15 mins)	re-asserts theme of lesson, clarifying topic
Writing begins and teacher goes round helping those she knows will be slow to start and any who ask for her help. Writing continues to the end of the lesson and is finished for homework. (30 mins)	INDIVIDUALISED TASK help to those needing it time for quiet task
Next lesson: some pupils' work is read and constructively discussed, followed by some exercise reminding them how to write direct speech which was something several did not get right in their work.	CONTINUITY FOLLOW-UP encouraging pupils and relating basic skills work to their own writing

Note There are several good points to this lesson apart from any mentioned above:
- it has a clearly stated theme
- it develops progressively
- activities vary (teacher-led talk, pupils' talk, shared reading, pairs work, individual writing)
- pupils have a lot to do and are kept involved, their experiences forming part of the content
- the teacher's role includes being a stimulator, guide, support
- talk, reading and writing are naturally interwoven
- clear examples and criteria are given for writing task
- not only are language skills used but the activities helped understanding and expression of feeling.

Activity 7:
Comparing types of lessons

There is no single kind of lesson format that could be called a good English lesson for all schools, teachers and pupils. The very breadth of aims and content discussed in Topics 1 and 2 demands that our lessons have variety, flexibility and space for spontaneity. This built-in flexibility cannot be properly indicated on a lesson plan. Nevertheless, it is instructive to look at some of the different possibilities for shaping lessons.

Below are three outlines of different kinds of lessons. Each class was mixed-ability and although each lesson makes use of all the language modes, they focus more on one than another (talk in lesson 1, writing in lesson 2, and reading in lesson 3). When you have looked at each outline, answer the questions which follow each of the lessons. These questions are to help you trace the steps the teacher took in planning those lessons.

Lesson 1: *3rd year Time: 1 hr 5 mins*

Aims:
(a) to make it seem natural to talk about experiences and share them with others
(b) to give practice in ordering the events of an incident into a narrative shape that will interest a listener
(c) to prepare for a writing task in a following lesson (in this lesson ideas are to be stimulated through anecdote and memory).

Organisation:
The teacher begins by telling the class about the time when, as a student, he was working on the post at Christmas; and about his encounter with a tramp who insisted on telling him his life-story. The teacher tells the class what the tramp told him and describes in lively detail what the tramp was like and how, as he told his story, he became fascinated by the tramp's character. After he has told the story he answers a few questions about it from the class.

Then he asks the pupils if they have ever had an encounter with a fascinating stranger or met someone who seemed a bit out-of-the-ordinary. He encourages pupils to describe their experiences and asks various questions that lead the pupils into further details.

After five minutes of this (just as more pupils are beginning to suggest they can remember similar incidents), the teacher puts them into groups of four or five and asks them to go round the group in turn telling each other of their encounters. This takes ten minutes or so; at the end he asks each group to decide which story in the group is the best for the rest of the class to hear. The selected member of each group then tells the class his story while the teacher encourages others to ask any questions to find out more.

After this there is a discussion to decide which of the stories is the one most suited to be the beginning of a story or novel about a stranger. Once the class has decided, the teacher tries to elicit from them the features of that story which make it interesting. He goes on to make a list on the board (taken from what the class tell him) of ways in which the opening of a story about a meeting with a stranger could be written. The list includes: mysterious atmosphere, a hint of danger, characters that the reader is likely to identify with and a character who is odd, perhaps frightening, and whose presence suggests something peculiar is about to happen.

The lesson ends with pupils copying the list down and being sent away to think how their own anecdotes can be changed to become the beginning of a story called *The Stranger Spoke*.

Questions

(i) How does this lesson vary its activities, and involve pupils in active learning, while still concentrating on a single language mode?

(ii) Is there anything about the organisation of this lesson which may not necessarily be successful?

(iii) How far does the shape of the lesson satisfy the stated aims?

Lesson 2: *2nd year   Time: 1 hour*

Aims:

(a) to help concentrate and focus on a scene in order to stimulate the imagination into creating a story

(b) to practise building up an imaginative piece of writing from a short, sharp concentration on perceptions and feelings. (This is to lead to a series of lessons in which pupils write, and look at their own poems.)

Organisation:

The lesson begins with the teacher reading from Scott of the Antarctic's diary, ending with the entry:

I do not regret the journey: we took risks, we knew we took them, things have come out against us, therefore we have no cause for complaint.

The reading is very moving and afterwards the teacher tells the class in more detail just how the tragedy happened, particularly the story of Captain Oates' sacrifice.

Then she asks them, 'What is the Antarctic like?' Instead of taking answers, she keeps them silent and makes them close their eyes and try to imagine it, recalling pictures they have seen. She stresses all the senses. Then she shows them photographs of the continent, pointing out all sorts of details. This is immediately followed by the class writing in rough a list of words and phrases which they feel describe what they imagine it is like. Some of these are read out and the most descriptive and detailed are put on the board.

The teacher takes what is on the board and reorders it, showing the class how to add words and images to create more detailed and lively descriptions of the snow, ice, wind, etc.

Then she says; 'Imagine you are with a team of scientists and explorers working on a survey of the Antarctic. You and five colleagues are away from base camp. The weather is fine; clear blue sky but very sharp, biting cold winds. The air is so cold that water droplets from your breath freeze into little icicles on your beard. But in your deep-lined parkas you are reasonably warm, at least until you get back to camp. Suddenly, as you are about to set off for base for the night, the wind changes direction and increases. A blizzard can be seen on the horizon. It is coming across your path, between you and the camp, and one of your colleagues is complaining of terrible pains in his stomach. Write down your thoughts, feelings and fears as you plod back towards camp, pulling your sled of equipment and knowing that as night comes down, a blizzard will make you lose your way and that would be the end of you all in a very short time.'

She warns them they have only ten minutes to do this and during that time she plays Vaughan-Williams' evocative *Sinfonia Antarctica* in the background.

When the ten minutes are up, she asks them for key words and phrases that they are using to describe the situation. Some are written on the board and again she shows them how these can be developed and tightened into sharper, more precise language. Then she asks them to work in threes, each of the three reading the rough work of the other two, and suggesting where the description could be improved.

After fifteen minutes of this they are asked to write individually a description or account of the situation they have been building up called *Alone in the Antarctic* or *Below Zero*.

Questions

(i) Why does this teacher take such pains to describe the scene to them?

(ii) Why does she put their ideas on the board? What effect do you think it might have to show them how to develop their ideas?

(iii) Why does she have them work in threes?

Lesson 3: *5th year Time: 1 hr 5 mins*

Aims:

(a) to encourage close reading of a text
(b) to help understanding of the topic of prejudice. This lesson is the first in a three-week theme on prejudice in which a wide selection of prose and poetry, and a variety of talk, writing and drama will be used.

Organisation:

Note:

There are no black children in this class.
The teacher gives copies of the poem 'Telephone Conversation' to each pupil and reads it to the class without any prior comment, other than to ask them to decide who is talking to whom.

     The price seemed reasonable, location
     Indifferent. The landlady swore she lived
     Off premises. Nothing remained
     But self-confession. 'Madam,' I warned,
5   'I hate a wasted journey — I am African.'
     Silence. Silenced transmission of
     Pressurised good-breeding. Voice, when it came,
     Lip-stick coated, long gold-rolled
     Cigarette-holder pipped. Caught I was, foully.
10 'HOW DARK?'... I had not misheard... 'ARE YOU LIGHT
     OR VERY DARK?' Button B, Button A. Stench
     Of rancid breath of public hide-and-speak.
     Red booth, Red pillar-box. Red double-tiered
     Omnibus squelching tar. It *was* real! Shamed
15 By ill-mannered silence, surrender
     Pushed dumbfounded to beg simplification.
     Considerate she was, varying the emphasis —
     'ARE YOU DARK? OR VERY LIGHT?' Revelation came.
     'You mean — like plain or milk chocolate?'
20 Her assent was clinical, crushing in its light
     Impersonality. Rapidly, wave-length adjusted,
     I chose. 'West Afrian sepia' — and as afterthought,
     'Down in my passport.' Silence for spectroscopic
     Flight of fancy, till truthfulness clanged her accent
25 Hard on the mouthpiece. 'WHAT'S THAT?' conceding
     'DON'T KNOW WHAT THAT IS.' 'Like brunette.'
     'THAT'S DARK, ISN'T IT?' 'Not altogether.
     Facially I am brunette, but madam, you should see
     The rest of me. Palm of hand, soles of my feet
30 Are a peroxide blonde. Friction, caused —

>   Foolishly madam — by sitting down, has turned
>   My bottom raven black — One moment madam! — sensing
>   Her receiver rearing on the thunderclap
>   About my ears — 'Madam,' I pleaded, 'wouldn't you rather
> 35 See for yourself?'

(Wole Soyinka)

The teacher asks a few questions to elucidate some of the language and make the scene clearer, e.g. 'What did the black man ring up about?' 'What country does it take place in?' He also concentrates on explaining lines 12, 16, 23-24, 33.

The pupils are given a worksheet to work on in pairs with various questions about the meaning of the poem including such questions as:
Why do you think the speaker decided to phone?
What do you think are the feelings of the black man at lines 4-5, 11-14, 27-32, 34-35?

After the worksheets are completed, the teacher goes back to a whole class discussion about the possible feelings between the two speakers and then has the pupils write down in dialogue form the actual words spoken in the poem. Then he asks each pair to rehearse how the poem can be read aloud to show exactly who is speaking and what their tone, feelings, etc. were. He ends by getting several pairs to read out the poem again and letting the rest of the class vote on which pair are most successful in conveying the relationship of the speakers.

The lesson ends with the teacher asking the class to describe the landlady's attitude towards the caller. When he receives the answer, 'Prejudiced', he asks them to say why they call it that. With a pupil's answer of, 'Because she didn't know nothing about him but she had already decided that because he was black, not because she knew anything about him really, she just didn't want to have anything to do with him,' the lesson ends.

Questions

(i) Why might the teacher use a worksheet rather than ask questions of the whole class?

(ii) Why does he get them to write down the dialogue in the poem?

(iii) Why does he get them to read the poem aloud themselves?

(iv) Why does the teacher not introduce the idea of prejudice himself at the beginning?

From aims to objectives

No lesson plan makes sense without some sort of pre-specified outcome, a clear aim. How we describe that goal to ourselves can affect crucially the successful outcome of our teaching.

What is the most practical way of expressing aims in a lesson plan? It is hardly enough to guide us if we express them at this level of generality:

>   to stimulate the pupils' imagination

or:

>   to improve critical thinking about a test.

What is required is to specify what we want in terms of *what we will ask the pupils to do* in the lesson, or what they should know or have practised by the end of the lesson. This is to state an objective. An aim is a high-level statement of intent; an objective is the precise information, skill or behaviour that we wish to see learnt or experienced through the activities we choose to include in the lesson. And it is most useful to think of these objectives in terms of what the *pupils* do rather than what the teacher does.

Activity 8:
Formulating objectives

Imagine you are planning lessons for a first year on the topic of *Animals and Man*. Your overall aims for a sequence of lessons are given below. Write what you think would be three objectives that will help you operationalise your thinking. (To do this activity it will be necessary to have in mind some of the kinds of resources you might use.)

AIMS (a) To help the pupils realise that man has a responsibility towards animals;
      (b) to use the familiar idea of pets, zoos, working animals, etc. as a basis for developing pupils' skills in describing things accurately and communicating their experiences to others.

SOME OBJECTIVES
1

2

3

For further study

Choose one of the following themes and design a sequence of lessons on it, suitable for a first or third year class. Don't plan the lessons in detail. State your objectives and indicate the kinds of activities each lesson will entail.

Possible themes: My neighbourhood Dreams/fantasy
                      People   What's funny?
                      The senses   Other worlds

**Topic 4
CLASSROOM
ORGANISATION**

Section A The classroom climate

The opportunity for learning is enhanced if the climate in which pupils are taught is conducive to active, participatory learning. English is a subject in which pupils are continually asked to express their thoughts and feelings, to make a personal response. This will happen only when a pupil has the feeling that his teacher respects him enough to listen to him tolerantly and responsively and talk to him with genuine attention. Such an attitude on the part of the teacher does not preclude clear and effective standards of classroom discipline, although it does demand a discipline that is not wielded in an authoritarian manner. The English teacher must create a classroom atmosphere which enthuses his class with a desire to read, write, and talk; which stimulates activity and signals an expectation of involvement, variety and pleasure. The classroom appearance and the teacher's role should combine to signal to the pupil that he is not going to be a passive receiver of someone else's wisdom, but an active maker of meanings under the interested guidance of an enthusiastic teacher.

Every classroom has its own atmosphere which reflects its teacher's interest and commitment level and which indicates by subtle signals just what he/she thinks the subject offers and what he or she expects of his pupils. This atmosphere is a product of both the physical environment and the teacher's role (attitude to pupils and way of organising a lesson).

**Activity 9:
Taking stock of
classroom climate**

Below are descriptions of two English classrooms in the middle of a lesson. Decide what the physical environment of the classrooms and the teacher's organisation of the lesson will suggest *to the pupils* about (a) what kind of a subject English is, (b) what is expected of them as learners, (c) what the teacher's attitude is to them. Enter your comments in the space provided after each description.

Classroom 1

A low-ceilinged, modern room with one wall entirely windows so it is light and fresh. A large whiteboard and tables, not desks, with pupils sitting four to a table. Cupboards are locked, there are no bookshelves. A few books on teacher's table; the odd exercise book and some battered texts not collected from a previous lesson. The walls are blank except for a peeling poster advertising winter sports. The class is in the middle of a comprehension exercise working from a textbook with questions after an extract. The pupils are working alone and the teacher, after reading the extract to them and asking a few questions intended to check that they have understood the difficult words and phrases, has told them to work in silence. When the occasional muttering occurs the teacher tells them to be quiet and work on their own, getting very angry with one boy who got up off his chair to borrow a rubber. The teacher sits at his table most of the time, keeping his eye on behaviour and immediately commenting on anything anyone does that might create a disturbance. The work goes on to the end of the lesson and they are given homework to finish it.

Your comment on the climate in this classroom:

Classroom 2

A Victorian beamed ceiling high up over a large slightly echoing room that is dark. A large old blackboard with one half converted into a noticeboard which is covered with various 'For Sale' and 'What's On' notices put there by the pupils. Pupils' work is displayed in several places, together with posters advertising book clubs, theatre visits, or hints about writing. On one wall there is a huge poster of 'knock-knock' jokes that the class have designed, collected and mounted. There are a lot of books around, including class library and reference books and anthologies. The teacher's desk is covered in books and papers which she is obviously using and not just left there forgotten. In this lesson the pupils are working in small groups answering some questions that arose earlier after the class as a whole had been talking about a video of a TV programme on the poet Ted Hughes which they watched last lesson. In their groups they are looking at a poem by Hughes and trying to decide what it is about. Soon they will report back to the rest of the class, and then their teacher will give them another poem and ask them to decide what questions they would ask Ted Hughes if they had been interviewing him for TV and wanted to throw light on this poem. This is part of a series of lessons on Hughes' poetry. The noise sometimes gets too much and the teacher quietens them in no uncertain manner but with some comment like, 'As you're near each other you don't have to shout.' She goes round the groups listening, joining in or explaining something.

Your comment on the climate of this classroom:

The best climate for learning in English is created by the atmosphere of the classroom as a kind of language workshop, a place in which the teacher has the space and flexibility to vary his or her own and the pupils' roles according to whichever approach and activity is most suitable at any one time. It is a workshop where the physical environment is capable of being changed to match the variety of activities (e.g. where chairs can be brought to form a semi-circle round the teacher for a concentrated reading activity), and where the teacher's relationships with the class are open, encouraging, respectful and helpful enough to promote an emotional climate where learning is a shared and desired end.

Activity 10:
Some classroom features

The following is a *selective* list of a number of features of the English classroom. Say what each feature might make the pupils feel about the teacher's expectations of the subject, of the pupils, and of the kind of learning he anticipates in his English lessons. Tick those features you think ought to be the ones promoted in your own classes.

Features	Expectations aroused in pupils	Features to encourage
straight rows of single desks		
plain, bare walls		
plenty of reading material around classroom		
each lesson varied in activities		
outside visits and visitors regularly		
pupils' work displayed		
pupils often involved in *doing* as much as listening		
teacher does not like mistakes		
teacher keeps strict order, constantly nagging, sometimes hectoring individuals		
teacher keeps order but not always quiet, except when someone is speaking to all class at once		
teacher is encouraging and tries to make pupils improve on past work		
teacher constantly compares pupils one with the other in effort to shame lazy and less interested into better work		

Activity 11:
Keeping control

Section B Discipline

Despite what the papers say, few pupils are violently disruptive in schools. Most everyday problems of indiscipline are unspectacular. Nevertheless, they are cause for action. The keeping of order or the reinstatement of order is always necessary if disorder threatens the likelihood of learning taking place.

Here are four typical everyday threats to order. What action would you take if you were the teacher and why? You may find it helpful if you can carry out this activity with a small group of colleagues.

Situation 1 It is your third lesson with this 3rd year class. You have been talking to them for 10 minutes and now set them to write individually. You didn't ask for complete silence. No one individually is making too much noise but the overall chatter is getting louder, and it's difficult to tell how much work is being done. Two boys at the back have not been paying a lot of attention and are now joking too loudly.

Suggested approach

Situation 2 You have been talking to a 4th year CSE group for over half an hour. You don't have too many discipline problems with them usually, but they often seem rather sulky, silent, even apathetic — especially when you want them to answer questions. This lesson they are particularly, irritatingly unresponsive. They don't appear to be listening; some are making signals at each other covertly, a couple are messing about with pens, another fiddling with his bag, a couple looking out of the window.

Suggested approach

Situation 3 The class are handing over their homework. All but three have done it. Of those who haven't, one was away last lesson, one usually does his, but the third has been late persistently. On previous occasions his excuses seemed vague. When you ask him why it's not done this time he says 'I forgot to take my book home.'

Suggested approach

Situation 4 This is a noisy 3rd year. You have been teaching them for two terms and know them well. Some lessons go better than others; most of the class will work if they are pushed hard and kept busy. There are a few who are resentful and antagonistic, particularly Kevin, whose work is poor and behaviour disruptive (staffroom rumour suggests his parents are in the middle of separating). In this lesson you are telling him off when he replies very rudely in an undertone, which is nevertheless heard by most of the class.

Suggested approach

Order is necessary for learning to take place. But that order should be the minimum required to let you and the pupils get on with the job and should stem from a discipline that is fair and reasonable. Rules should be explained, and routines established, in such a way that their purpose is *understood* by the pupils as being to give everyone an equal chance of working and not as being a reflection of an arbitrary authority of the kind implied in 'Do that because I said so.' Your discipline is based on the authority of knowing your subject and being skilled in the methods of teaching it. There should be no room in schools for authoritarian tyranny. That is not to say that you can be 'soft' with pupils. Pupils expect and desire authority, but they want *rational* authority. Creating good discipline is, more perhaps than any other aspect of learning to teach, something which requires practice and experience. However, because it is made up of the exercise of particular skills, it is possible to benefit from reflecting upon what these skills entail before you enter the classroom. There are several useful books concerned with how to manage your class of which these are the most helpful:

    E.C. Wragg, *Class Management and Control* (Macmillan, 1982)
    M. Marland, *The Craft of the Classroom* (Heinemann, 1975)
    W.J. Gnagey, *Motivating Classroom Discipline* (Macmillan, 1981).

There is no reason to assume that the English classroom throws up any discipline problems that are different from those in other subjects. There is only space here to remind you of ten essential steps towards increasing your awareness of possible disruptions in your class and how to exercise your management to avoid these becoming intolerable.

Essential steps towards classroom control

1. *Prepare lessons thoroughly*. Aims and methods should be decided before the lesson starts. But have alternatives in mind too, including follow-up activities for those who work faster and finish early. Have all resources ready and distribute books and materials efficiently.

2. *Keep the class busy*. Avoid monotony by varying activities and building up a lesson of different tasks in several stages. Do not talk for too long at a time. Changeover from one activity to another is a time for disruptions, so do it smoothly and quickly. Make all instructions clear and simple. Give instructions *before* letting pupils do a task and be prepared to repeat them without feeling irritated.

3. *Be alert to everything that goes on*. When you talk to an individual pupil don't forget to keep looking up to see what others are doing. Use your eyes and ears all the time. If pupils think you notice everything, you won't have to comment on every little piece of inattention or indiscipline.

4. *Organise lessons* so that you proceed from the simple to more complex ideas/skills and arrange for the majority to be successful at each stage.

5. *Watch for signs of inattention and boredom*, and if one or two are affected let them know you have spotted them. If large numbers are affected, *change* the lesson by altering timing or placing of tasks. Deal gently with minor misdemeanours but make sure the offenders know you are aware of them. If they persist, make an example of selected individuals. Always use names to make the individual feel it's him/her you are speaking to.

6. *Make as few rules and routines as possible*, but check that they are understood and stick to them.

7. *Make requests or commands in a civilised but firm manner*. Avoid shouting as much as possible, so that when you have to raise your voice you know they will be alarmed. *Simulate* anger if it helps occasionally

but never really lose your self-control. Avoid unnecessary threats. If you make a threat make sure it is one you are prepared and able to carry out. Have a ladder of action: start from just raising an eyebrow and looking determined, and go through to the biggest sanction the school allows (always make sure you know the school's accepted sanctions).

8 *Praise and encourage whenever you can*. Praise works better than criticism in getting pupils to improve. Sometimes private comments to persistent offenders after a lesson is over works better than a public humiliation.

9 *Begin fairly strictly with a new class and ease up later*. Start formally. Be scrupulously fair with no favourites or perennial victims. No nagging, no revenge, no sarcasm! Be prepared to have your leg pulled but don't be over-friendly. Pupils' respect is gained by: good humour, fairness, a desire to listen and help, willingness to explain, patience, firmness, consistency and expertise.

10 In case of persistent trouble (a) isolate and deal with ringleaders, (b) talk to another member of staff about your problems.

TOLERATE MISTAKES IN PUPILS AND YOURSELF. LEARNING ARISES FROM ERRORS.

Section C Some organisational skills

Collecting ideas and resources

All teachers require sources for ideas about the topics they will teach. For the English teacher, seeking appropriate topics, sources and resources is a major skill because the content of English cannot be limited to any set syllabus or course textbook. While thematic anthologies may be useful at times, there are none that can provide all the material you need. A steady flow of ideas for books to use, topics and themes to explore and sources of new experiences to consider is the lifeblood of English. English does not have to be a continuous bombardment of original and stirring stimuli, but variety of content and approach is the only way to give interest and motivation and to cover the multifarious meanings of language at work.

The English teacher must be a jackdaw when it comes to gathering materials and sources, prepared to seize any bright idea from wherever or whomever it arises. In the hectic activities of everyday teaching it is easy to fall back on the stock-cupboard's contents. But teachers who wish to expand their own and their pupils' horizons will always be on the look-out for a wider range of resources. Bearing in mind what is appropriate to their pupils' age, ability and attitude, they will have a mind, ear and eye alert for any interesting possibilities for new lessons. Such teachers will be inveterate collectors and hoarders of items stored away for future lessons not yet planned. It is useful to remind yourself just how diverse a range of ideas can be used:

Possible sources for lesson material

Print	*Non-print*
novels and stories	photographs
poems	paintings
plays	any kind of material object
newspapers	guests and visitors
colour supplements	visits
magazines and comics	music of all kinds
biography and travel	TV, radio and film
brochures, instructions and forms	the work of other pupils

Indeed, almost anything we experience can provide that spark which lifts our imagination and helps us conceive a topic worth introducing to our class.

Activity 12: Collecting ideas

A simple test of your ability to be imaginative in your collection of ideas and resources is to collect ten sources for just one topic. Over the next week or so, write down here the ten items (print and non-print) you can get together to use to illustrate one topic of your own choice.

TOPIC......................

1........................... 6...........................
2........................... 7...........................
3........................... 8...........................
4........................... 9...........................
5........................... 10..........................

Teaching mixed-ability classes

Variety of resources is a benefit to all types of teaching, and variety in all aspects of teaching is the key to handling mixed-ability classes. All the activities described in this book are suitable for such classes. Only remedial work is not touched upon here because that demands specialist knowledge, and there is not the space to cover it in a book of this kind. A good starting point for considering such work in English is to be found in R.W. Mills *Teaching English Across the Ability Range* (Ward Lock, 1977). More general books are to be found in the DES Focus series advertised on the cover of this volume.

One important point concerning mixed ability teaching in English must be made here, a point that should *underlie all the thinking and planning you are asked to do in this book*. It is that everything you say and do should take account of the individual differences between pupils — their diversity of cognitive ability, language skills, and speed of assimilation of new ideas. There are several ways in which you can cope with this diversity:

Lesson organisation in response to mixed ability

(i) *Grouping* Mixed-ability groups cannot be taught as a whole very often (except perhaps for reading something with them or talking about ideas for writing). It is useful to individualise tasks and make use of small group work. When using small groups in mixed-ability classes arrange for the poorer readers to be mixed with the better readers so that the former gain from the latter. Try to encourage the less able ones to contribute by giving them the opportunity to talk in these groups. The less able are often handicapped by their poor reading skills, and when given a chance to talk and do tasks orally are frequently the equal of the more able readers.

(ii) *Worksheets* Alternatives to whole-class teaching include using sheets that present tasks, activities or questions and contain all the information and instructions necessary for completing them. Pupils can work on their own, in pairs, or groups to answer them. Such sheets should be attractively produced with drawings, cartoons and diagrams as well as words. Some slower children grasp a point made by a drawing quicker than the same point verbally explained. The sheets can either be arranged in two to three levels of difficulty so that pupils of different abilities complete different work, or else the series of questions and tasks can progress from the simple to the more difficult and the least able are allowed to progress at their own speed.

This means the more able are stretched further but all complete the same basic work.

(iii) *Audio-visual aids* Since the less able sometimes pick up points more quickly from non-print cues, it is important to use audio-visual aids whenever you can. In any case, all pupils benefit from varying the type of stimuli. Try to use your imagination to devise supplementary non-print sources. An example could be recalling the relationships of characters in a novel by means of a diagram.

Beginning, timing and talking

Beginning

Even when an individual lesson is part of a linked series of lessons, it is important to structure it so that it has a clear introduction and conclusion which will point pupils towards your theme. Here are some practical points to bear in mind:
1. give out as many materials as possible before starting
2. check the pupils are comfortably seated (check coats, bags, etc. are out of the way)
3. signal the beginning forcefully and deliberately
4. don't begin until you have silence and attention
5. project your voice to the whole class and look at them as you are speaking
6. try to start with something that catches their attention or whets their appetite for the lesson.

Timing

Timing of activities needs to be such that a good flow of varied tasks occurs in each lesson. The activities could include listening to pupils recounting an experience, questioning, reading together, small-group work, writing, suggesting ideas for writing, rough work, final draft work. Furthermore, short steps in which there is a chance for immediate success and feedback, help sustain concentration. Very few activities should continue unmodified for more than fifteen minutes, especially with the less able. Keep up a busy pace but don't rush or confuse pupils. Make sure everyone knows exactly what is expected of them.

Talking and showing

Although English teachers probably spend less time talking to a class than teachers in some other subjects, a lot of time is still spent with the teacher standing in front addressing the whole class. It's important to remember that most things can be explained in other ways. Try, as much as possible, to keep pupils active. Even when you are questioning a class you can sometimes get them to write an answer down before hearing what they have to say. In this way, thinking is not restricted to the willing few. Whenever you can, *show* as well as speak.

This is particularly important when looking at a text or trying to set up a piece of writing. Direct pupils' attention to finding things in a text, and suggest writing by having as many examples as possible before they begin. Don't neglect the blackboard – it is an indispensable visual aid. Enliven your explanations with personal anecdote, frequent illustrative examples, metaphorical turns of speech and engage pupils in dialogue as often as possible and with as much good humour as you can!

There are many times when we do have to talk: explaining, recounting, informing, describing, instructing. So we must learn to talk with clarity, in a vocabulary appropriate to pupils' ability, with humour and liveliness of expression (a boring monotonous delivery soon sends an audience to sleep).

Section D Reading aloud

Reading to pupils occurs in nearly every English lesson. It is one of the most important skills for you to master. You need to read with enthusiasm, passion and dramatic vigour if you are to capture the interest and attention of your pupils. The ways to practise are to record yourself, or to have a colleague observe and evaluate you doing it.

Activity 13: Reading aloud

Get a colleague to sit and listen to you reading to a class, then ask him or her to fill in the evaluation sheet printed below.

Scale	5	4	3	2	1	Comment
Projection						
Clarity of diction						
Variety						
Speed						
Emphasis of meaning and mood						

Scale 5 excellent
 4 very good
 3 satisfactory, but lacking really forceful presentation
 2 unsatisfactory — you must practise to improve this particular quality
 1 totally unsatisfactory at this reading. Practise, practise, practise!

Explanation of criteria:

Projection: the extent to which you can 'throw' your voice and personality towards your audience and make them interested in listening to you. This is an absolutely vital skill and greatly affects not only reading to a group, but teaching them anything at all. You need to be able to hold their attention, if not their interest!

Clarity of diction: how far words and phrases are clearly enunciated. This doesn't require a particular kind of accent, but it demands that you are careful not to lose or destroy consonants at the beginning and ends of words (e.g. read *moving off* not *movin' off*). Also, don't swallow vowels in the middle of words. Clarity is related to speed. Read too fast and clarity will soon disappear.

Variety: the extent to which you avoid sounding monotonous. Levels of pitch and speed of delivery should vary according to the mood and sense of what you read. This is absolutely vital when reading poetry.

Speed: do you read too fast, or too slowly? Does the speed vary to underline mood, tone and meaning? Most beginners have a tendency to read too quickly. Remember, when your audience can't see the words you read, it is particularly important to slow down and give them thinking time, time to catch up with what you read.

Emphasis of meaning and mood: the above skills, properly observed, should give you this. To get it right means: (a) you should have read what you are reading *before* you read it aloud; and you should be sure you understand not only what it means, but how the writer achieves that meaning; (b) as you read aloud you should still be thinking all the time about the way each phrase should be expressed. Don't read in automatic gear.

Note If you read well to your class they are more likely to enjoy reading for themselves.

Part 2   TEACHING ENGLISH

You will spend many hours teaching during your career. During this time you should continue to work at your teaching skills like a craftsman, quite deliberately seeking to improve them.

Part 2 of this workbook contains nine activities during which you will focus on some particular aspects of teaching English and on skills appropriate to an English teacher. Ultimately you are responsible for developing and evaluating your own professional competence. If you are still at the training stage you are able to call on the help of your tutor, teachers in the school and fellow students. More experienced teachers are encouraged to get together in pairs with colleagues, or to work with several other teachers in a department or Faculty.

The nine activities in this workbook are arranged, in fact, so that you *have* to approach fellow students, fellow teachers or tutors to help you. Do not feel threatened when these observers offer you advice. In teaching there is always a great deal to learn, even if you are fortunate enough to possess certain natural advantages. In any case it would be boring if you felt you had already reached a state of perfection, with no prospect of improving. Most teachers are aware that in the cut and thrust of classroom life there are frequent opportunities for rethinking one's approach.

The purpose behind this workbook is to provide some structure and a framework of advice within which you can develop personally throughout your career. There is deliberate overlap in the tasks observers are given. It is useful to have more than one view of some aspects of your teaching, and there is much merit in encouraging a more open approach within the profession.

Timetable

You need to organise yourself so that each of the nine tasks is completed. For students this is in itself a very important part of your training. Poorly organised teachers often come to grief. Do not wait for someone else to jog you into action, take the initiative yourself. Explain what is involved to the relevant observer and work your way through the set. Remember to follow up in each case as suggested.

More experienced teachers may feel that the opportunities for this kind of systematic observation are limited. But the nine Focuses can be used quite separately and in any order. As a qualified teacher with experience upon which to draw you will know which of these nine tasks require your more immediate attention, given your personal circumstances.

Focus	Title	Who observes	Date completed
1	What's in a question?	You and a colleague	
2	Handling classroom discussions	You and a colleague	
3	Talk in small groups	You and a colleague	
4	Ways into a class novel	You	
5	Looking at poems	You	
6	Reading in bottom gear	You	
7	Planning for writing	You	
8	Structuring writing tasks	You and a colleague	
9	Responding to writing	You	

Focus 1
WHAT'S IN A QUESTION?

Introduction
Questioning is an essential skill for any teacher to possess. To be able to ask the kind of question that elicits an honest, interested and relevant response from a pupil is the first prerequisite of constructive talk in the classroom. The intention of this section is to help you consider the place and purpose of questioning, to familiarise yourself with the different types of questions, and to help you practise some of the necessary skills involved in questioning.

This Focus leads to the planning, teaching and evaluation of a lesson which relies heavily on questioning as a teaching strategy. It proceeds to this lesson through (a) considering the purposes of questioning, (b) reflecting on the different levels of questions, (c) practising the skills of questioning.

What to do Each part of this exercise should be undertaken in turn. Sections A and B should be done before planning your lesson. You should ask a colleague to observe your lesson using the criteria in Section C.

Section A The purposes of questioning
(a) A group of English teachers was asked to say why they used questions in their teaching. A list compiled from their replies is given below in random order. Place these functions in your own order of priority to reflect what you think are the most important purposes of questioning in your own teaching.

	to make pupils feel their teacher wants to know what they think and feel
	to recall information, etc. so the teacher can judge how much has been learned
	to discover what problems and difficulties are being experienced with a particular task
	to develop a hypothesising and problem-solving approach to learning
	to aid pupils' externalising and verbalising of what they know
	to help pupils learn from each other and respect each other's opinions
	to stimulate pupils' imaginations
	to check understanding of what has been read
	to improve pupils' ability
	to articulate response
	to change the direction of a discussion to more productive areas
	to arouse interest in a topic and stimulate the desire to know more
	to help pupils expand and elaborate their ideas
	to explore a topic and discover what pupils think about it

(b) On a separate sheet of paper, either give an example of a question, or describe the place in a lesson where a particular kind of question would be appropriate for each of the purposes described in the list. Wherever possible your example should be derived from a recent lesson you have taught or observed.

Example

Priority	*Purpose*	*Example*
5	to improve pupils' ability to articulate response.	After reading the poem 'Timothy Winters' ask class in groups of four to decide 'What kind of family background do you think Timothy comes from?'

Section B Types and levels of questions

Introduction As that activity indicated, the places within English where questioning can occur are many and varied. But wherever questions occur it is important for the teacher to be fully aware of the differing levels of thinking which different types of question will stimulate. A simple question requiring factual recall demands from a pupil a very different level of cognitive response from a question asking him to hypothesise or solve a problem.

Printed below is an extract from the novel *The Incredible Journey* by Sheila Burnford. A teacher was reading this animal adventure story with his first-year mixed-ability class as part of several weeks' work on the theme of *Man and Animals*. The extract is taken from the opening chapter. The teacher stopped his reading occasionally to question his class about a particular paragraph which he thought it was important they should understand fully if they were to follow the story. His stated purposes in questioning them were (i) to check their understanding of the text, (ii) to prepare them for later developments in the story, (iii) to encourage a personal response and to help them identify the story with aspects of their personal experience.

What to do Read the following paragraph and the questions the teacher asked his class. Remembering the purposes of questioning considered in Section A, *identify the function* of each of the teacher's questions and *write a brief comment explaining how effective you think each question would be* in eliciting a response appropriate to the function you identify.

On the floor, his scarred, bony head resting on one of the man's feet, lay an old white English Bull terrier. His slanted almond-shaped eyes, sunk deep within their pinkish rims, were closed; one large triangular ear caught the firelight, flushing the inside a delicate pink, so that it appeared almost translucent. Anyone unaccustomed to the rather peculiar points of bull terrier beauty would have thought him a strange if not downright ugly dog, with the naked, down-faced arc of his profile, his deep-chested, stocky body and whip-tapered tail. But the true lover of an ancient and honourable breed would have recognised the blood and bone of this elderly and rather battered body; would have known that in his prime this had been a magnificent specimen of compact sinew and muscle, bred to fight and endure; and would have loved him for his curious mixture of wicked, unyielding fighter yet devoted and docile family pet, and above all for the irrepressible air of sly merriment which gleamed in his slant eyes.

He twitched and sighed often in his sleep, as old dogs will, and for once his shabby tail with the bare patch on the last joint was still.

Questions the teacher asked

... What do you think 'translucent' means?
... What kind of dog is a bull terrier?
... How would you describe this dog, in your own words?
... Do you think the writer thinks he is an ugly dog?
... What sort of a life do you think this dog has had?
... What kinds of things does the writer tell us about the dog which makes us think the dog has been a fighter in his day?
... Just look again at the words and phrases used to describe the dog. Which ones do you feel really make us think this dog is a real character?
... Sarah says, "It makes me feel like he's a dog that doesn't need humans really." What do you think about that, John?
... Can you imagine anything about the story that is going to be told, just from what we learn about this dog? He's going to be the important character. Can you imagine what kind of adventure it might be?
... Now, how many of you have, or have had, a dog as a family pet?
... What we've got here is a detailed description of one dog, a dog very familiar to the writer, and he helps us imagine quite a lot about his distinctive character – you know, his personal characteristics that make him different from all other dogs. Think about a pet of yours

for a minute. Any kind of pet, not just a dog. Tell us some of the peculiarities it has – the way it looks or the funny little habits it has – those oddities that make it very individual. What kind of things do you remember about it?

Section C Practising your questioning skills

What to do   You should now plan a lesson to fit into any scheme of work with any class you are currently teaching in which a central part of the lesson will make use of a questioning strategy. In your plan note down the *key questions* you will employ to promote pupil talk and thought, and also the objectives you intend to achieve through the questioning. Ask a colleague to observe the lesson and write a brief evaluation in which he judges the effectiveness of your questioning against the following three criteria:

Observer's evaluation criteria

(a) Were the questions clear, capable of being answered, and at a level of language appropriate to pupils' level of comprehension?
(b) How effective was the questioning in promoting pupil talk (i.e. replies longer than a short phrase)?
(c) Was there a variety of levels of cognitive demand made upon the pupils?

Some essential questioning skills

As you plan and teach your lesson bear in mind these important practical points:
... Address individuals by name as much as possible;
... Aim for a wide distribution of questions, spreading your attention to all;
... Allow thinking time; pause after asking a question and take more than one answer before commenting on what is said;
... Try to avoid answering your own question!
... Pay attention to the level of language; always aim for clarity, simplicity, and avoid ambiguity or questions that are too complicated;
... Vary the thinking level demanded; try to move towards some questions requiring reasoning, some seeking personal response, some problem-solving, etc.;
... Ask supplementary questions to help pupils expand and elaborate their first answers;
... Give plenty of praise and encouragement;
... Ask supplementary questions that prompt and give clues when the going is difficult;
... Create a climate where exchange of views is natural; encourage pupil-participation.

Follow-up

1 For your next lesson try to plan questions with a view to building up *a sequence of questions* that progresses carefully from simple to more complex, from recall to reasoning, from concrete particulars to more abstract and general questions. Discuss your plan with a colleague and then after he or she has watched you teach the lesson, decide between you how successful you were in leading your class through a productive thinking process via your questions.

2 You will find helpful practical advice in the following:
Trevor Kerry, *Effective Questioning* (Macmillan, 1982)
Michael Marland, *The Craft of the Classroom* (Heinemann, 1975), pp. 74-76
L. Cohen & L. Manion, *A Guide to Teaching Practice* (Methuen, 1983), pp. 245-8, 282-91

Focus 2
HANDLING CLASS DISCUSSIONS

Introduction

Now, I want us to talk about abortion. Let's discuss some of the issues. Right, then, Sandra, let's begin with you. Do you think abortion is a good idea?'

SILENCE FROM CLASS.

It is not a travesty of the classroom situation to suggest by this quotation that there is something artificial about the teacher's role in class discussion or unresponsive about the pupils' reactions.

A discussion is an exchange of views, opinions, feelings and ideas in which the participants have an equal opportunity to express themselves. Discussion in a classroom under the direction of a teacher is inevitably a more formal affair than a spontaneous exchange of views between friends in a pub. The constraints reflect the fact that within a classroom such discussions have the over-riding aim of helping pupils to learn. In the English lesson there is the further aim of teaching pupils the actual skills of communication. It is not only the content of talk but also the manner in which we conduct ourselves in discussion that is being learned.

So discussion with large groups in English has to start from the fact that it is a *controlled* learning experience, directed by a teacher, but it should be organised in such a way that the necessary formal constraints do not prevent the creation of a climate in which pupils feel able, and are willing, to contribute and enter into a free exchange of views.

What kinds of discussion are possible and what kinds of skill do they demand from the teacher? The following activity is intended to help you answer these questions.

What to do Prior to teaching a lesson making use of discussion you should fill in the examples in Section A. Then plan and execute a discussion as outlined in Section B. This section requires a colleague to observe and comment upon your lesson.

Section A Reasons for holding class discussions

Complete the following, giving examples from your own lessons of each numbered reason.

1 Exploring a topic arising from shared reading and leading towards a writing task
   Examples:

2 Talk leading to some form of action (e.g. planning a visit; simulation)
   Examples:

3 Clarifying issues of a controversial nature (e.g. abortion; disarmament)
   Examples:

4 Building pupils' confidence in holding their own ideas/opinions
   Examples:

5 Helping pupils to argue from evidence and to respect opposing views
Examples:

6 Talk leading to decision-making (e.g. agreeing rules for a class society)
Examples:

7 Developing ideas, sharing experiences to stimulate written work
Examples:

Section B Assessing your skill in handling discussions

(a) Choose a topic from your current teaching and plan a lesson in which you feel it would be appropriate to your aims to spend part of that lesson discussing a topic with the class as a whole. Write down your purpose in starting such a discussion, noting the time you hope to devote to talk and any points of organisation you consider essential for the proper conduct of the discussion. Explain what your role will be in leading the discussion. Hand your notes and lesson plan to a colleague who will observe that lesson.

(b) After the lesson both you and the observer should complete the following checklist and discuss your separate observations. Under each numbered teaching point indicate how you think the skills mentioned were evident.

1 Was the topic presented clearly and were instructions unambiguous?
Your response:

2 Was a climate created in which pupils felt able to give opinions?
Your response:

3 Did the teacher show himself or herself sensitive to the feelings of pupils and willing to listen?
Your response:

4 Did he/she ask open questions (to which there were many acceptable answers) rather than closed ones?
Your response:

5 Did he/she avoid dominating with his personal views?
Your response:

6 How many pupils participated?
Your response:

7 Did the pupils respect others' opinions?
Your response:

8 Were minority opinions protected?
Your response:

9 Did the teacher introduce information, evidence, reading material, etc. at appropriate points?
Your response:

10 Were pupils encouraged to give evidence for their views?
Your response:

11 Were digressions permitted?
Your response:

12 Was a clear structure provided?
Your response:

13 Were too many ideas raised?
Your response:

14 Did the teacher provide a summary at the end?
Your response:

Follow-up

Over your next few lessons examine your discussion with classes and try to ensure that pupils have the opportunity to do the following:

... put forward speculative ideas
... judge for themselves the evidence in an argument and draw their own reasoned conclusions
... try to provide evidence for a point of view *opposed* to their own
... use ideas originating from a discussion in a piece of discursive writing.

Focus 3
TALK IN SMALL GROUPS

Introduction

A discussion with the whole class is not always the best way of getting pupils talking. Shy and less confident pupils can hide from the teacher and not necessarily contribute. With lively or awkward classes such discussions pose discipline problems. A useful alternative for promoting productive talk is the use of pairs or small groups of pupils (not larger than six) combining to talk and work on a specified task.

The following different small-group situations were set up in three separate lessons by the same teacher in one day's English teaching:

(1) a 4th year in groups of four deciding how they would tackle the problem of football hooliganism, and then coming together in a whole class discussion about the nature of soccer violence.

(2) a 3rd year in groups of three to five looking more closely at the poem 'Pike' by Ted Hughes. Each group was asked to answer a different question on the poem before they all came together to pool their ideas and complete an overall response to the language and meaning of the poem.

(3) a 1st year class in pairs trying to build up the plot for their own ghost story after reading a ghost story in class and before writing a class story.

The advantages of such small group work are:

... the shy, nervous and slower learners feel more secure and more likely to contribute among their peers;
... a relatively informal and secure atmosphere creates more confidence in handling ideas;
... the language of a friendly group imposes fewer constraints on speaking;
... more pupils have the opportunity to contribute so that active, participatory learning is encouraged;
... pupils have more control over the direction, pace and purpose of the talk.

What to do Decide on an activity which could be approached through small-group work. Using the hints in Section A, plan an activity of no more than fifteen minutes using pairs or groups of 3. Teach this lesson and arrange to tape the discussions of one of the groups.

After the lesson listen to the tape and draw your conclusions as to the effectiveness of small-group talk by considering: (a) the quality of pupil response, (b) the level of language and thought, (c) the amount of pupil participation, (d) the quantity of productive talk.

Do you consider this activity has advantages over whole-class discussion or question-and-answer strategies? Why? Discuss this with a colleague.

Note If your class is not used to being recorded you may have to do this experiment two or three times before you get a natural result.

Section A Organising groups

When organising your groups, bear in mind these points:
1 *Try friendship groups*; keep to groups of three or four at first and give a strict time limit.
2 *Give specific instruction* (perhaps written); specify the outcome and prescribe the structure without predetermining the content.
3 *Provide a central focus* (e.g. something to read or a decision to be made).
4 *Encourage note-taking* by all group members.
5 *Arrange for groups to report* back to the rest of the class and exchange views.

Follow-up

1 In later lessons experiment with your own role. *Remember*: it takes time and experience to get the best from working in small groups. Try these differing strategies:
... go round each group trying to encourage and question, and join in;
... stay the whole time with just one group (not as chairman but just as another member);
... do not go round groups.

Pay particular attention to the quality of the pupils' work arising from these different strategies and see if you can form a judgement as to the relative merits of each approach. Discuss this with a colleague.

2 To judge the role and importance of small group work it is useful to examine transcripts of pupil talk. Examples can be found in:

D. Barnes, *From Communication to Curriculum* (Penguin, 1976)
J. Britton, *Language and Learning* (Penguin, 1972)
R. Mills (ed.), *Teaching English Across the Ability Range* (Ward Lock, 1977)

**Focus 4
WAYS INTO A
CLASS NOVEL**

Introduction

Reading the same novel with a whole class provides a common experience, a shared response to a text. It's not the only kind of reading that should be provided and promoted in the English lesson but, handled with sensitivity, it can be an important and enjoyable way of introducing the delights of reading fiction. The aim of reading fiction with pupils in class is, firstly, to stimulate wider voluntary reading for pleasure – to hook kids on books – and, secondly, to improve pupils' ability to read with understanding and appreciation. Although entertainment through reading is an early aim, it is closely followed by the aim of providing opportunities for readers to explore their sense of reality through the imaginative recreation of experience offered by good-quality fiction. It is the English teacher's responsibility to provide such fiction, and to devise ways of helping pupils to reflect upon their response to a text through talking and writing about topics suggested by their reading.

The following activities are intended to help you (a) consider how to organise the reading of a class novel, and (b) to construct an extended scheme of work that will promote that 'shared response to the text'.

What to do These two activities are planning exercises to be done prior to using a set novel with your class. The planning is appropriate for any novel being read with ages 11-15. Section A concerns the way you will actually read the novel with the class; Section B provides you with a framework for helping pupils reflect upon what they are asked to read, without burdening them with critical analysis too early.

Section A How to read a novel with a class

The checklist below is designed to help you make decisions about organising the reading of a novel. As you work through the list, decide what is most appropriate for you to do with your particular class and tick the relevant item on the list when that decision has been made:

1 How will you read the novel with your pupils?
   (a) teacher reads the whole story aloud
   (b) all pupils take turns in reading sections aloud
   (c) selected pupils only take turns in reading
   (d) teacher reads major part but some pupils (volunteers) read brief sections
   (e) a combination of reading aloud (crucial incidents) and silent reading

2 How long do you intend to spend reading the novel?
   (a) one or two lessons each week (remaining lessons on other English)
   (b) every lesson until the novel is finished (other English temporarily suspended)

3 During reading how much attention will you give to understanding language?
   (a) is there a need to provide context (historical, social/political, genre, etc.)?

(b) how often will you stop to explain/ask questions about difficult words/phrases . . .
   (i) as they occur?
   (ii) at the end of chapters and natural breaks in the story?
   (iii) only when lack of understanding prevents the story being followed?

4 What follow-up work will you need?
   (a) activities required to link pupils' experience with subject and theme of story
   (b) character studies (development, relationships, conflicts, etc.)
   (c) use of crucial incidents as stimuli for exploration of a theme (e.g. opening *Great Expectations* as a prelude to thinking about what it is like to be afraid)
   (d) activities designed to help pupils identify with characters' situation

5 Is your scheme of work on the novel designed to:
   (a) concentrate just on the novel?
   (b) use the novel as umbrella for all English work including language skills, writing, talking, drama, etc.?

Section B Constructing a scheme of work on a novel

To be sure of giving your class time and opportunity to reflect on their response to the novel, it is necessary to plan ahead a scheme of work that will make them look more closely at the crucial events in the plot, the nature and relationships of the central characters, and the developing theme of the story. To achieve this you should plan a sequence of activities that use talk and writing to explore the meaning of the story.

Your aims might include:
1 improving understanding of the plot
2 helping identification with characters (putting pupils in others' shoes)
3 exploring relationships between characters and linking these with pupils' own views of life
4 appreciating some of the ways the author expresses, explores and communicates his or her view of his characters and their situation
5 using the novel as springboard for pupils' own consideration of topics raised by the story.

Below you will find a sample scheme of work arising from one teacher's use of *Carrie's War* by Nina Bawden. This novel was read with a third-year class. The teacher decided which were the crucial, critical events in the story, and asked himself what it was about each of these events that his pupils needed to understand if they were to get the most from their reading. Then he planned a series of activities to help them achieve that understanding through talking and writing in relation to the novel.

Study this scheme. All the main events in the novel are listed, followed by a *sample* of the desired learning targets associated with two events, and an *example* of the classroom activities related to one of the learning targets. When you have studied it *plan a scheme of work associated with your choice of a class novel*.

Critical events of the plot

1. Arrival in Wales, meeting with Mr Evans and sister, Lou and their first night as evacuees.
2. The visit to Druid's Bottom and the frightening walk.
3. First meeting with Hepzibah and Mister Johnny. Is Hepzibah a witch and Mr Johnny mad? Their surprising kindness and puzzling ways.
4. Some light on Mr Evans: Carrie gets to know more about his attitude to Mrs Gotobed and the people at Druid's Bottom.
5. Before and after Mrs Gotobed's death: Carrie meets her and is told something she doesn't understand. Lou goes away and comes back with some new habits that infuriate Mr Evans. Mr Gotobed goes and a question mark hangs over the future of Hepzibah and Mr Johnny.
6. A farewell tea at Druid's Bottom; Carrie throws away the skull and fears something terrible will happen.
7. Lou elopes with her 'fancy man', leaving Mr Evans. Carrie learns more about Mr Evans and his past, understands the reasons for his mean and miserable attitude.
8. Druid's Bottom burns down and Carrie believes it's a result of her throwing away the skull. Years later she returns as a mother herself with her children and meets Hepzibah and Mr Johnny once again.

Learning targets
(a sample)

1. (a) to understand the reasons for evacuation.
   (b) to imagine the atmosphere of the Evans's house and what it was like for Carrie and Nick.
   (c) to understand the characters of Carrie, Nick, Mr Evans and Lou.
   (d) to visualise the circumstances in which they lived at the house/shop.

5. (a) to be aware of Mrs Gotobed's character, reasons for the breach between her and Mr Evans.
   (b) understanding the effect of this on Mr Evans's attitude and his Calvinistic religion.
   (c) implications for the Will and its consequences.
   (d) introduction of the theme of responsibility and obligation towards others.

Classroom activities
(an example)

1. (a) (In groups) list the rules of the Evans's household (written from Mr Evans's point of view as if pinned up on the children's bedroom door).
   (b) (in pairs) Write a newspaper report for a local paper commenting on evacuees' arrival in Welsh valley:
      – why evacuated
      – who organised and helped in village
      – what type of person evacuated (use Mr Evans)
      – quotes from evacuees (Albert: 'It was like a cattle auction')
      – in-depth interview with Mr Evans. (This could also be done as role-play.)
   (c) Drawing of the Evans's house and shop and a written description of the village.
   (d) Discussion and written profile on Lou's and Mr Evans's characters using the following list:
      outgoing – shy
      talkative – quiet
      generous – mean
      happy – miserable
      sympathetic – unfriendly
      stable – moody
      timid – bold/bullying
      disorganised – rigid
   (e) Diary entry by Carrie recounting their first night at Mr Evans's.

Focus 5
LOOKING AT POEMS

Introduction

The anxiety that sometimes arises among English teachers about using poetry in the classroom is a result of several factors, but two of the most prominent are: the assumption that pupils will reject poetry as 'wet', and the fact that teachers who themselves are widely read in poetry are in the minority. Children presented with poetry as a natural part of the other reading and writing they do will accept it quite willingly, provided that it is not made the object of a literary critical crossword puzzle. Poetry that is about a life that they can recognise will be as welcome as any other kind of literature. This Focus is not a complete guide to using poetry in the classroom, but it suggests some general principles to help you plan a lesson that centres on looking at a poem.

What to do In Section A you are asked to plan a lesson you can teach to any of your classes, using Ted Hughes's poem *Wind*. This poem is chosen because it can be read at several different age levels. Section B is a post-lesson self-evaluation. Do not look at it until after you have taught the lesson.

Section A Planning to use a poem

The following poem could be used in various ways. Let us assume that on this occasion your main aim is to help your pupils see how the poet makes words work for him to recreate the experience of being in an isolated house in the middle of a storm.

To achieve such an aim you have (a) to give pupils an opportunity to relate the situation, events and feelings expressed within the poem to their own experiences; (b) to help them see for themselves some of the techniques by which the poet selects and arranges his words and ideas. If both (a) and (b) are achieved, you will help your pupils to respond to the poem as a natural extension of putting experience into words and to understand the tools by which a poet handles his language. But, remember, it is the pupils' response to the poem's subject that should come first; and it is only to reinforce this response that we touch on any kind of analysis. If the analysis irritates the pupils, or forms a barrier rather than a bridge between them and the poem, it is a waste of effort.

The poem is printed here with boxes to indicate some of the features (diction, sound, rhythm, imagery) that you might wish to help your pupils to see. One or two examples have been entered in the boxes, the remainder are left blank for you to fill in. There are also questions at the end of the poem for you to answer. After doing that you should plan and teach the lesson in which you intend to make this poem the focus.

WIND

This house has been far out at sea all night,
The woods crashing through darkness, the booming hills,
Wind stampeding the fields under the windows
Floundering black astride and blinding wet

Diction: what is the effect of key words in creating mood?

Till day rose. Then, under an orange sky,
The hills had new places, and [wind wielded
Blade-light, luminous black and emerald
Flexing like the lens of a mad eye.]

Alliteration: effect of repeated sounds

At noon I scaled along the house-side as far as
The coal-house door. I dared once to look up:
Through the brunt wind that dented the balls of my eyes
The tent of the hills drummed and strained its guy-rope.

The fields quivering, the skyline a grimace,
At any second to bang and vanish with a flap:
The wind flung a magpie away, and [a black
Back gull bent like an iron bar slowly.] The house

[Rang like some fine green goblet in the note
That any second would shatter it.] Now deep
In chairs, in front of the great fire, we grip
Our hearts and cannot entertain book, thought,

Or each other. We watch the fire blazing,
And feel the roots of the house move, but sit on,
Seeing the window tremble to come in,
Hearing the stones cry out under the horizons.

Contrasting images: humans grasping what comfort there is against natural elemental forces. Precarious position of man. *Theme*?

NOTES

1 The poet has said he was most concerned to express 'the strength of the blast; the way it seems to shake the world up like a box of toys'. How exactly does he achieve a recreation of that sensation?

2 How will you help your pupils to see that this is what Hughes is doing? What kinds of experiences of their own could you get them to talk about that would help them appreciate Hughes's aim?

3 Here are three alternatives to doing a strict analysis of the poem but which might be useful in helping pupils understand and appreciate the poem (each could be undertaken by a small group and answers shared):
(a) imagine you are a TV video editor and you have been asked to edit a sequence of images to accompany a reading of the poem so as to reinforce its mood. Write your cutting list describing what images you want to use (include details of camera angles and time sequence)
(b) prepare to read the poem aloud deciding how to vary speed, tone and mood, and how to bring out the most meaning. Tape your reading.
(c) List all the things the wind is likened to and decide *exactly* what characteristics of the storm each comparison is intended to recreate.

Section B Putting the poem into a lesson

Answering these questions should help you judge how far you managed to (a) give the poem a context natural enough to overcome any pupil-resistance to poetry, (b) guide pupils into an *active* personal response, (c) make them aware of the poet's intention, techniques and level of achievement.

(i) What context did you use to introduce the poem? How far did you relate its subject to pupils' own lives?
(ii) Which questions were the most productive in eliciting pupils' responses? Why?
(iii) Were all your questions to the whole class or did you also work in pairs, small groups, individually?
(iv) If you did have any talking or writing that went beyond whole-class discussion what advantages (if any) do you think it had?
(v) What features of the poet's creative use of language did you highlight?
(vi) What kinds of pupil response do you feel you aroused?
(vii) If you used this poem again with a similar group, what changes might you make to your lesson and why?

Follow up

Try using poems in the course of your next few lessons, introducing them in as natural a way as possible. As you do so, bear these general points in mind:

1 You must be a regular reader of poetry yourself and familiarise yourself with poetry suitable for your pupils (particularly contemporary poetry).
Have books of poems in your classroom, particularly good anthologies (you will find a guide to these in S. Tunnicliffe, *Poetry Experience* (Methuen, 1984).
2 Remember that your aim is always enjoyment and interest before analysis. Try to demystify poetry (it should not be thought of as outside pupils' experience) and don't kill off personal response by premature dissection. Books that are readable and contain useful creative exercises for helping you and your pupils to get inside poetry in an enlivening way are *The Practice of Poetry* by Robin Skelton (Heinemann, 1975) and the book by Tunnicliffe mentioned above.
3 Instead of 'concentrating obsessively on a rarified selection of "excellent" poems, we should show that poetry can fulfil all the purposes of stimulating prose, and more. It can amuse, move, disgust, convince, teach and record' (T. Evans, *Teaching English*). Look beyond lyric poems and use humorous verse, riddles, ballads, etc.
4 The way into poetry is through talking, reading and writing which in different ways lead pupils to see that each word has to work for its place in a poem. Why is it this word and no other? Attention to the associative meanings of words, to their sound and rhythm, are all ways of helping pupils to the inside of the craft of writing.
5 This leads naturally to pupils writing their own poetry. This should begin with imitation and modelling of simple forms (haiku, proportional verse, etc.) and by playing with words so that pupils come to see them as 'plastic', capable of being turned into a variety of shapes to recreate an experience, insight, mood or emotion.
6 'Poetry writing, and to a lesser extent reading, become easier if poetry is presented as a craft, a series of skills which can be taught or practised.' (Evans, *op. cit.*) A gradual introduction to the characteristics of poetic language and structure (especially sound, rhythm, pattern, diction and imagery) is necessary.
There are several very practical books that will give you ideas for looking at poetry as a craft:
Sandy Brownjohn, *Does It Have to Rhyme?* and *What Rhymes with 'Secret'?*
 (Hodder, 1982)

B. Powell, *English Through Poetry Writing* (Heinemann, 1968)
Ted Hughes, *Poetry in the Making* (Faber, 1967)
S. Tunnicliffe, *Poetry Experience* (Methuen, 1984)

BUT REMEMBER TO READ POEMS SOMETIMES JUST FOR THEIR IMMEDIATE IMPACT, RHYTHM, IMAGERY, DEVELOPMENT OF MOOD OR IDEA — FOR PLEASURE!

Focus 6
READING IN BOTTOM GEAR

Introduction

Without doubt, the first aim of reading with pupils is to pass on to them the pleasure to be derived from books. But the classroom is a focus for learning and not a division of the leisure industry, and one of the essential elements in learning to read for pleasure and profit is acquiring the skills to reflect upon the meaning of a text — to recognise its purpose, understand what is said, be sensitive to what is implied, to appreciate and evaluate its significance. Traditionally, English teachers have sought to pass on these skills of close reading through comprehension exercises. Often this means giving pupils written questions to test their understanding of a short extract from a longer piece of writing. It is a slowing-down of the normal reading process in order to check that the reader has grasped the details of the meaning and significance of the passage. However, such exercises can all too easily become boring and ineffectual when they ought to be profitable and stimulating. There is no doubt that teaching pupils to drop down a gear so that they can reflect on a text and actively question the writer's intention, his or her attitude to his or her subject, and the effects of the language used, is a vital reading skill. The following activity will enable you (a) to be clear about the skills you should be developing through close reading activities, (b) to devise comprehension work that will not degenerate into a series of isolated and sterile exercises, (c) to try your hand at planning an exercise in 'reading in bottom gear'.

What to do You should undertake the activity in Section A before planning and teaching your own comprehension lesson as described in Section B. To gain the most from this Focus, the follow-up should be regarded as an essential part of the activities you are asked to undertake.

Section A The skills to be developed

Coursebooks in English usually include passages with suggested questions to test pupils' comprehension of the extract. Select such an extract from a suitable coursebook and decide if the accompanying questions test whether the pupils can do the following:

1 *Word skills* — recall and deduction of meaning of key words, phrases, sentences
2 *Literal understanding* — locating significant ideas; summarising and paraphrasing such ideas
3 *Deduction* — following the main sequence of ideas, understanding relationship of ideas
4 *Evaluation* — drawing conclusions; forming judgements; assessing value or truth of passage
5 *Appreciation* — recognition of attitudes, tone, structure and style of passage

Section B Designing your own comprehension activity

Choose a suitable extract, devise your own questions designed to elicit all five aspects of reading skills, and then plan and teach a lesson in which you make use of this exercise. In selecting the passage and thinking about your questions bear the following teaching points in mind:

1 Select extracts that are long enough to be interesting (perhaps you might read out a longer passage and just reproduce part of it for the closer reading task).

2 Provide a context for the passage, linking it with a topic of interest to your pupils.

3 In recognition of the individual differences in ability, start with simpler questions based on literal understanding, follow on with questions that require pupils to show how they can follow a sequence of ideas, and finally, provide questions (or tasks) that demand a demonstration of powers of reasoning and deduction from the pupil. Not all questions should be at the level of recall and repetition of what the writer meant.

4 Permit the expression of personal opinion to encourage individual response to the text (e.g. 'Do you agree with the writer's view that . . .? Why?' or 'Would you have done that in x's circumstances?').

5 Present additional questions designed to stretch the ablest pupils.

6 Consider talking over some questions before asking for written answers.

7 Plan for some questions/tasks to be done in pairs or small groups.

8 Include a final question/task leading to a longer piece of writing connected with the theme of the extract and the context in which you placed it.

Use this *planning guide* to help you plan your lesson.

What factors influence your choice of a passage?

How will you provide a suitable introduction and context?

Plan the questions and/or tasks for the different levels of understanding:
Level 1 (word meanings)

Level 2 (literal understanding)

Level 3 (deduction)

Level 4 (evaluation)

Level 5 (appreciation)

Which questions/tasks might be suitable for small group work?

Will there be any talk or discussion prior to, or during the exercise?

Will you present the exercise on a worksheet? If so, why?

What further tasks will you undertake to provide continuity?

Follow-up

There are alternatives to this traditional form of comprehension. You will find detailed descriptions of them in K.Gardner & E. Lunzer, *The Effective Use of Reading* (Heinemann, 1979). Three alternatives are briefly described below. Try to utilise them over the next few weeks of your teaching.

1 *Cloze procedure* Present a text with every tenth word (or key words of your own choice) deleted, apart from in the first and last paragraph. Pupils in small groups are then asked to decide what the missing words are. It is not essential that they should predict the original words — suitable synonyms will be acceptable providing the original meaning of the text is upheld. This activity gains its validity from the *reasoning* and discussion that goes into coming to a decision. Context cues and anticipation skills (the essentials of fluent reading) are practised.

2 *SQ3R* Teach your pupils to
survey a passage (pick up the most important clues enabling them to 'tune in' to the content in the shortest time);
question it (what do I already know about this subject? Where is the evidence for this statement? What is the writer's attitude? — preparatory questions that will guide the reader towards a critical view of what he is reading);
read it (closely, attending to all implications);
review it (look back over it to discover gaps in what has so far been picked up);
recite it (prove to themselves that they understand it).
This activity is also best done in pairs or groups.

3 Further group exercises are:
Prediction: a passage is cut into several separate paragraphs and presented in the order in which it was originally written. Ask the pupils to try their hand at deciding what is likely to come next. To do this seriously means using all the clues from the previous paragraph that lead them into perceiving the development of an idea.
Group sequencing: the cut-up paragraphs are presented to a group in random order and they are asked to decide on the correct order of the original text. Here, again, it's not the right answer that matters but the process of discussing and analysing the ideas in the text which leads to a close reading and an active interrogation of the text.

**Focus 7
PLANNING FOR WRITING**

Introduction

'I can't say I always like it but I suppose it makes me think more.' (Third year boy)
Not all our pupils welcome the amount of writing they are asked to undertake in our classrooms, but writing is nevertheless an indispensable language experience for every pupil. The reason for this becomes obvious if we ask ourselves what writing offers that speech cannot provide.

Writing differs from speech in at least these ways:

1 It has no immediate audience to provide feedback on the success of our

communication and therefore requires the message to be explicit and precisely elaborated.
2 It allows time for reflection, for second thoughts, revision, etc.
3 It provides a chance to look back and check our communication for inaccuracy, inconsistency, ambiguity and incompleteness.
4 'Whereas talk is evanescent, writing leaves footprints.' It permits a permanent record for an audience separated from the writer by time and space.

These differences provide us with an awareness of the functions that writing may perform in our classroom. According to one group of English teachers who were asked 'Why insist so much on pupils writing regularly?', the act of writing provides:

(a) opportunity for sustained thinking and reflection by an individual
(b) clarification of ideas and a record for future reference
(c) a means of exploration and discovery of pupils' opinions, ideas and feelings;
(d) satisfying a desire to *make* a pleasing verbal artefact, something consciously shaped for a specific purpose;
(e) the practice of technical skills
(f) the means to check whether something has been thoroughly understood.

If writing is to fulfil these functions the teacher needs to bear in mind certain principles:

... provide a variety of different types of writing on a wide range of subjects (see Section A below)
... provide a climate which encourages pupils to draw on their own experience for ideas;
... pupils differ in their approaches to a task and their speed of working, so planning must allow for this by giving additional tasks to 'fast finishers' and leaving room for individuals to plan and execute their work;
... writing tasks should vary in the quantity demanded — not all writing should be as long as a story or essay;
... spend time on developing ideas with pupils before they begin writing — examples should be shared, and talking and reading activities should be carefully linked with what you ask pupils to write;
... practice in the craft of writing (structuring ideas, patterning, developing particular moods/tones, using figurative language, elaborating vocabulary) must be a regular part of the build-up to longer writing tasks;
... avoid premature insistence on correctness of grammar, which can demotivate pupils and destroy their confidence that they have anything to write.

What to do Below is a list (not complete) representing the scope of the possible modes of writing. Study this list and enter in the right-hand column an example of each mode that you could undertake with your classes — some examples are already given. Then go on to complete the planning task in Section B.

Section A Types of writing

Types	Example of classroom activity
story (narrative) creating incident, settings, characters, etc.	
diary (personal and expressive)	
essay (formal organisation of ideas)	
letter (personal and public formats)	

report/record (objective account of events in the outside world)	account of football match
autobiography	
instructions/explanations (informing, conveying data, etc.)	conjuring trick
discursive (discussion of issues)	
persuasive (changing someone's view)	for/against bloodsports
creative (including poetry — imagination needed to pattern experience and provide pleasing aesthetic object)	
descriptive (object, places, people, etc. based on close observation)	visit to dentist recreating atmosphere and expressing feelings

---

Section B Planning writing activities

Choose any three different types of writing tasks from the previous section and make an outline plan of a lesson intended to get your class undertaking such a task. Plan your lesson with its sequence of activities in the following format.

Lesson 1   Writing mode:

Development of lesson:

Lesson 2   Writing mode:

Development of lesson:

Lesson 3   Writing mode:

Development of lesson:

The following are helpful teaching points:

- a key moment in writing tasks comes when you move from talking to a class to launching them into individual writing. Don't become taken up with help for individuals in the first five minutes of writing, but instead concentrate on keeping everyone under scrutiny, damping down distractions and answering urgent questions.
- some pupils find beginnings especially difficult. Try to help them find starting points or provide additional ideas, or get them to work in pairs, or provide an alternative perspective/assignment. Some useful ideas for getting started are to be found in R. Protherough, *Encouraging Writing* (Methuen, 1983), pp. 125-129.
- go round, helping individuals, trying to get them to *talk* about problems. Give them confidence in their own ideas and encourage them. Don't limit yourself to correcting language errors — help with content, approaches to material, etc.

- encourage the use of rough notes, rewriting and going through drafts.
- decide what to do about early finishers; e.g. rewriting? elaborating ideas? reading their work to others? different work? reading? corrective work from earlier writing?
- avoid simply instructing the class to finish off for homework. Give precise instructions. (Homework is best for collecting ideas, rough drafts or making notes — so long as all are utilised in the lesson.)
- give time for proof-reading before handing-in. This is the opportunity to correct obvious careless slips and technical errors.

Follow-up

After you have taught your three lessons, write a brief report in which you comment on these points:

1 What was the function of this piece of writing? Did you make the purpose clear, relevant and interesting? Did it connect with other activities?

2 What audience did the writing assume? Were you able to provide readers other than yourself in the role of assessor (e.g. other pupils, parents, outside adults)?

3 What quality of response did you get? Does the quality of the pupils' writing suggest they found it difficult or straightforward?

Focus 8
STRUCTURING WRITING TASKS

What to do Plan a lesson on a chosen topic that leads to asking your class to do a piece of continuous writing of some kind. Pay close attention to the stages in the writing process outlined below in section A. Teach the lesson with a colleague acting as observer, and then discuss your own evaluation with your colleague. The lesson observation/evaluation is outlined in Section B.

Section A Stages in the writing process

Writing is a difficult task. Too often we assume that, after giving pupils an initial stimulus to arouse interest in a topic, we can simply leave them to complete a story, essay or poem. But even the professional writer has to make plans, use notes, reflect on issues and then go through several rough drafts before completing his final publishable draft. Pupils who are still learning *the process of thinking through writing* require help from their teacher with regard to how to organise their ideas on paper. What kind of help can we provide?

It is possible to identify several stages in the process of moving from initial idea to the final written draft. These stages are outlined below. After you have studied them you should plan your lesson in detail, trying to include activities that enable you to take your pupils through these stages.

		Objective	Method
1	*Starting points*	presenting a subject, giving stimulus and creating impact	possibilities include *reading* something with pupils; *talking* about personal experiences; *talking* about some incident from daily life, news, local events; photographs, films, videos; *listening* to tape, music, radio; *looking* at an object
2	*Talk around the subject*	providing a focus	the theme of the writing should gradually emerge from this

3	*Providing an example*	gives a model for writing	either an extract from professional writing or an idea drawn from the class and built up on the board to show how the writer achieves the effects and what techniques are necessary
4	*Exchange of ideas*	*from class* helps motivation to write and reflect on the subject	important to *involve pupils* and develop their suggestions so as to give them confidence in their own ideas. This is also the stage when preliminary notes might be made.
5	*Help with structure*	shows how to order and develop ideas	this should be connected with examples and make use of pupils' ideas. To give them some sort of pattern/shape to aim for in their work. May include: writing parts on board; showing how to expand and detail ideas; providing signposts as to what to include in paragraphs etc.
6	*Writing*	(i) rough draft first (ii) teacher comments and encourages by reading some aloud (iii) revision/editing before: (iv) final draft (v) proof reading (for basic errors of language)	Remember: a writing task need not necessarily demand a long piece. It could be short to practise a particular skill (e.g. story openings). Longer work might be attempted step-by-step rather than asking a class to write a complete piece at once. During writing you can go round speaking to individuals suggesting how they might proceed. Give plenty of support and encouragement.
7	*Responding*	not just marking but also reading pupils' work to rest of class: display work in some form	Praise whenever possible. Show how even good work can be extended, elaborated, etc. Identify any problems with basic skills and remind pupils of relevant rules.

Section B Evaluating your lesson

(a) When you teach the lesson you have just planned ask a colleague to observe you and the class. During the lesson your colleague should try to answer the questions in the *Observer's evaluation* list.

(b) After you have taught the lesson try to sum up your impressions of how it went by asking yourself the questions in the *Teacher's evaluation* list. Then discuss your impressions with those of your observer.

Observer's evaluation

1 Did the opening of the lesson capture the interest of the class?
2 Did the pupils contribute ideas and talk around the topic?
3 What evidence was there that the class understood precisely what was required of them in the written work?

4 Was sufficient help given to enable the class to draft their initial ideas in rough?

5 From the questions pupils asked, comments they made, etc., what kinds of difficulties do you think they encountered with the writing task?

Teacher's evaluation

1 How much contribution did the pupils make to the lesson?

2 What amount and quality of ideas did I get from the class?

3 Did I provide enough help for them to shape their writing?

4 Did I explain clearly the kinds of things I was looking for in their writing?

5 What kinds of help did they ask for when I started them on the final stage of the writing?

Follow-up

1 Even this amount of help may be insufficient for the slower learners in a mixed ability class. What further help might they be given? In considering them it is important to bear in mind the following:
- make sure they are drawn into any discussion (consider using small groups)
- try to take an example for writing from someone you know usually has difficulties, and elaborate that idea in front of the class, suggesting how it might be turned into a workable written piece
- when the class begin writing individually, seek out those you know find it hard to get started and talk to them about their ideas, concentrating on getting them to feel confident about the worth of their own suggestions
- when choosing to read out work in progress or final drafts to the rest of the class don't overlook what is offered by the less able pupils.

2 The drafting habit is time-consuming yet it is a crucial factor in improving pupils' efforts. Try to establish it as a habit in much of your work. In doing so bear these points in mind:
- it is necessary to teach pupils how to make notes. Ensure that final drafts are not just rough-book work written out again word for word.
- talk and reflection are vital steps between first notes and writing a rough draft. Show pupils how to expand and elaborate their first ideas. Try to get them used to thinking beyond the first idea that comes into their heads.
- don't neglect attention to vocabulary and choice of words
- if you ask for both rough drafts and final drafts to be handed in and you demand to see a change and development between the two, you should quickly establish the idea that rough work is not just done to make it easier to spot spelling and punctuation mistakes
- rough drafting is about developing ideas, not correcting errors in basic skills (that is done at the proof-reading stage) and for this to happen you need to give time to this part of the writing process.

You will find some practical hints on the use of drafting in:

Robert Protherough, *Encouraging Writing* (Methuen, 1983)

Donald Graves, *Writing: Teachers and Children at Work* (Heinemann, 1983)

A. Dewar, D. Jackson, E. Millard, *Working with Third Years*. Available from The English Centre, Dept of Education, The University, Lougborough, Leics. LE11 3TU (£1.00 postage included)

P. D'Arcy, *Writing: A Voyage of Discovery*. Available from P. D'Arcy, County Hall, Trowbridge, Wiltshire.

**Focus 9
RESPONDING TO WRITING**

Introduction

A great deal of writing is demanded of pupils in English and the first point to emphasise concerning assessment of that writing is that *NOT ALL WRITTEN WORK SHOULD BE MARKED*. As we saw in Focus 7, we set written tasks for a variety of purposes not all of which are best served by a teacher's grade being awarded. It may be enough simply to check that certain rough notes have been done, or to have something read out by pupils in front of their classmates, or just to reward what has been written by an individual by giving her a word of praise or encouragement. A teacher's response to writing should clearly encompass more than the award of a numerical grade. Yet, inevitably, we must sometimes grade a piece of work and mark it in a full sense.

When we do, what kinds of general principles must we work to? Two particular principles seem vital if we accept that responding means more than marking out of 10 or 20:

... responding involves not just assessment of success but also diagnosis of particular strengths and weaknesses;

... responding means providing help and encouragement: helping the writer to do even better next time and encouraging him or her by praising whatever is successful in respect of his or her past work.

The following activity should help you to put these principles into operation.

What to do Section A alerts you to the sort of questions you must ask yourself before approaching any marking. This section should be carried out over two weeks of teaching. Section B helps you to look closely at a particular piece of your own marking and should be undertaken when Section A is complete.

Section A Approaching your marking

During two weeks you should have a number of pieces of written work handed in by your classes. As you mark this work, consider the list of questions which follow, and try to formulate answers relevant to the particular purposes of the writing tasks you set, the kind of help you gave to the class in structuring that writing, the criteria of success you gave them and the knowledge you have of those pupils. By considering these questions, you should make yourself much more explicit about the way you will respond to written work, while remaining flexible over the exact criteria to apply to any single written task.

Criteria	*Comments*
What am I *looking for* most of all in this work?	
What is my *priority*? — originality of ideas — liveliness of expression/style — accuracy of basic skills — presentation	
Written comment on pupils' work: what is its purpose?	

does the tone and style in which it is written matter? If so, why?

Attitudes to *basic skills*:

which mistakes in spelling, punctuation, and expression should be marked?

in what way should such errors be pointed out?

Attention to *expression & style*:

in what way will you point out successes and weaknesses?

how do you hope to develop pupils' best work?

Giving *help and encouragement*:

will you include written comments to do this?

will you point to details with positive comment, ticks etc.?

Returning work to pupils:

will you read out and comment on examples?
will you speak to individuals?
will you show examples of successful work?
will pupils share each other's work?
will you have corrective work done in class?
will you use this work to lead into new work?

Section B Marking exercise

Choose three different types of written task that you will give to your classes. Before marking the work, assess your procedure using the following checklist. Then do your marking and decide for yourself which criteria implied by this checklist are most appropriate for your particular purposes.

	Tick if appropriate to tasks		
	1	2	3

What are the purposes of your assessment?

Diagnosing language problems of individuals

Monitoring pupils' progress

Screening out individuals for special help

Stimulating ideas

Improving clarity of expression and communication

Any other purposes?

Different levels of marking

Intensive (marking all major language errors as well as commenting on ideas, etc.)

Impression (not picking up every error but awarding mark, and making comment based on overall impression)

Response (not giving literal or numerical grade but written comment including your *feelings* about the piece of work)

Focal (singling out particular criteria to check on — anything from punctuation to liveliness of ideas and style)

Handling in class

Examples to be read in class

Corrective work (basic skills, etc.) to be done in following lesson
— individually
— as class

Comment orally to pupils
— individually
— as class

Explanation to class of criteria used in marking

Are any grades to be given on basis of:
— relationship to past performance of pupil
— your understanding of standard for this age
— what is normally expected of *this* class?

Will you give a grade for *effort* (i.e. good, satisfactory or unsatisfactory commitment and hard work) as well as *achievement*?

TREAD CAREFULLY. Remember the effect on pupils. ENCOURAGE RATHER THAN CRITICISE.

Follow-up

1 Mark a class set of written work and select a sample of six individual pieces to represent the full range of your marks. Get a colleague to assess these six without seeing your marks or comments. Encourage him to include corrections, any comments, etc. as well as a mark. Afterwards discuss your respective assessments, concentrating particularly on any mismatches.

2 Read the practical advice on marking given in A. Stibbs, *Assessing Children's Language* (Ward Lock Educational, 1979) and Pauline Chater, *Marking and Assessment* (Methuen, 1984).

Part 3

REFLECTIONS ON EXPERIENCE

Topic A
REVIEW OF TEACHING

If you have carried out the Focus activities in Part 2 you have had a chance to practise some key skills of organising English lessons. This topic is a self-evaluation exercise to help you judge your level of success in the classroom and plan future lessons.

Activity 14:
Looking back over lessons

Select two lessons you taught recently enough to remember in some detail how they developed. Select one that you consider relatively successful, and another that you regard as unsuccessful. Answer the following questions as honestly as you can, applying them to each lesson in turn.

Then write a report (on a separate sheet of paper) trying to sum up what you feel to be the most important things you have learnt about your role as teacher, the outlook of your pupils, and the nature of your subject.

If you can, discuss your evaluation with a colleague who undertakes the same task. Be as honest as you can and share your successes, doubts, worries etc.

Remember: 'From error to error we proceed towards truth'!

What were your aims in the lesson selected?

Having taught the lesson, would you want to change those aims in any way?

Remembering the way the lesson developed, note below each of the following headings anything you consider was a key factor in the success or otherwise of the lesson:

Choice of topic

Introduction/stimulus

Overall organisation/method

Exposition/questioning

Class discussion

Pupil activities in groups/pairs/individually

Textual focus

Writing (structuring or setting)

General climate/atmosphere in classroom

Relationships with pupils

Behaviour of class

If you were to teach this lesson again to a similar class what changes would you make?

Activity 15:
Achieving continuity and balance

One of your concerns in reflecting upon your teaching will be to check for a balanced programme in your lessons. It is necessary to aim for a varied programme in which there is a balance between all the *language modes* and all the possible *approaches* to the subject, and a continuity between *activities* (varying between individual, small-group work, and whole-class tasks), *stimuli* (visual, auditory, actual experiences as well as the written word), *genres* (poetry, plays, novels, non-fiction, etc.), *teaching roles* (as explainer, guide, questioner, instructor, coach, leader, fellow-learner) and *levels of demand* according to the age, ability and attitude of your pupils.

A popular way to plan for such continuity and balance is to teach by theme or extended project. A general subject area (anything from 'Man and Animals' to 'Things That Go Bump in the Night') which is capable of arousing pupils' interest and active response, is chosen to provide the link between a series of lessons lasting anything from a week to a term. Under this subject all the different kinds of English activities are gathered. In this way, it is hoped that:

... isolation of individual lessons is avoided and a coherence is given instead to the various language experiences which we give to pupils;
... the topic permits several different perspectives enabling work to be varied enough to motivate very different sorts of pupil.

This activity cannot tell you how to fully organise a theme. The kinds of activities and skills already covered in this book will remain the centre of your individual lessons even under a thematic approach. What this activity does is to take you through the stages of choosing a theme and the initial overall planning of a scheme of work.

Follow through the suggestions below, ticking off each one as you complete the thinking, decision-making and planning required.

1 *Choosing a theme*

   Select a topic that is wide enough to make connections between many different approaches;
   Select a topic capable of imaginative approach, not based too heavily on factual data (one allowing personal, affective base); must be appropriate to age, ability of pupils.

2 *Collecting ideas (coverage and aims)*

   List every possible idea and source material you can think of.
   Examine list and place in order of priority of most productive ideas.
   Decide what you hope pupils will discover, learn and practice.
   List range of activities and skills you want to cover.

3 *Method (learning activities)*

   For each approach, source and idea, decide pupil activities.
   Decide which activities are best done individually or in groups.
   Decide how and where you will use worksheets.
   Decide how classroom will be organised.
   Summarise sequence of lessons with topics and ways of working.
   Check range of skills pupils will cover individually.
   Decide your role in each lesson.
   List sources and aids you will need to gather before you start.
   How will you begin the theme?

4 *Presentation and outcome*

   What form will pupils' work take?
   Decide what kinds of presentation, display, publication are intended.

5 *Checking learning (keeping a record)*
   Decide how you will record pupils' progress.
   What form of assessment will you use?

   (See *Topic B* for record-keeping.)

Follow-up

1 After you have taught the theme, review its success with your class, asking them and yourself:
- did the theme approach give them more chance to find a personal way into the work?
- did they have a sense of variety and unity?
- what things proved most difficult, boring etc. for them?
- what did they enjoy and find useful?
- what kinds of subject interest them most?

2 Practical help in planning themes can be got from Mills (1977), Stratta (1973) [see bibliography], and P. Scott, *Coursework in English* (Longman, 1983).

**Topic B
KEEPING RECORDS**

'Teachers' markbooks should be more like notebooks than scoreboards.'
A. Stibbs, *Assessing Children's Language*

Apart from marking and assessment procedures (dealt with in Focus 9), which may well be determined by the policy of individual schools or departments, all English teachers need to think about their means of recording the progress of their pupils.

Records are the footprints of a pupil's progress, and should chart not only what he has achieved but also where he has travelled through. Our markbook should be a repository not only of marks but also of the kind of work that has been done and a diagnosis of individuals' needs. In this way the markbook becomes a compilation of pupil profiles and a record of what the teacher has been doing.

Some functions of record-keeping:

... recording marks/grades for individual assignments ... a summary of written comments on pupils' work	record of pupil progress
... identification of areas/skills requiring further work ... a check on balance of activities so far undertaken	information for future teaching
... general assessment of pupils' attitudes, relationships with teacher and other pupils	record of social development

**Activity 16:
Compiling a profile of pupils' progress**

Set out below is an example of a profile of pupils' progress as kept by one particular teacher (adapted from R.W. Mills, *Teaching English Across the Ability Range*, 1977). There are two parts to the profile. One is a record of writing, talking, reading and social skills (right-hand column) and the other is a detailed profile of a single pupil's language competence (left-hand column).

Make a similar chart in your own markbook (adding or altering any of the categories) and fill it in as your teaching progresses through a term or year. Use the chart

... to give you information about individuals' strengths and weaknesses
... to decide what kinds of work you need to develop to retain a balance between the different kinds of language experience pupils have
... to form the basis for discussions about progress with pupils, parents or colleagues.

Example of an individual profile

Name: John Smith		
Comprehension		
little or no understanding		
grasps only main points	✓	
understands most of his reading		
full understanding at his own reading level		
Oral		
(a) Class discussion:		
takes no part unless asked directly		
occasionally has something to offer	✓	
ready to join in discussion		
partakes fully in class discussion		
(b) Language:		
barely grammatical		
grammatical but poor vocabulary	✓	
tries to use more interesting words		
fluent and interesting		
Written		
(a) Content:		
puts very little on paper		
tries but lacks originality — poor vocabulary	✓	
good standard, reasonable vocabulary		
good fluent work, original content, wide vocabulary		
(b) Grammar:		
lacks sentence construction		
writes in sentences but little else		
fair use of punctuation and grammar	✓	
very good construction and grammar		

Example of part of a class record

Mary White	Kevin Brown	Janet Jones	David Smith		
				Reading Comp.	
				Quantity	Writing
				Presentation	
				Spelling	
				Punctuation	
				Structure/Style	
				Vocabulary	
				Imagination	
					Oral, including Drama
					Breadth of Reading
					Class Readers Studied
					Other Remarks (e.g. Behaviour, Contacts with Parents)

Topic C
WHAT IS GRAMMAR?

'They don't teach grammar these days, so it's no wonder kids can't write.'

This not uncommon attack on English teachers rests on two assumptions, both of them mistaken. The first assumption is that what was taught as grammar in the past was valuable; the second assumption is that knowing grammar helps children write more effectively. What used to be taught as grammar consisted of a description of parts of speech, clausal analysis, syntactical rules and a series of prohibitions (e.g. 'Never end a sentence with a preposition'). It is difficult to imagine in what way learning this could prove to be of value, unless it does help children to write more effectively. A great deal of research has been done to see if this does happen and the overwhelming conclusion (see summary in A. Wilkinson, *The Foundation of Language*, Oxford, 1971) is that, at best, it has no such effect and, at worst, actually confuses children and writing skills are adversely affected.

A further confusion exists in the minds of those who regret the demise of this kind of grammar teaching. Many use the label 'grammar', to mean not the rules of language use so much as the basic functional skills of spelling, punctuation, etc. Now, if it is being said that the command of such skills is helpful in teaching pupils to write, then something important *is* being said. Such skills are a vital component of the English syllabus, to be taught when the need arises, i.e. when pupils display *specific* weaknesses (see Focus 9).

Does this mean that there is no room for teaching pupils something about grammar? Certainly there seems no justification for formal teaching of grammar. However, there should be room for doing something to improve children's awareness of some grammatical nomenclature, and certainly a need to promote greater awareness of the social attitudes to language (e.g. accent and dialect).

Activity 17:
Encouraging language awareness

Below are some suggestions of topics you might include at almost any stage of an English syllabus and which are intended to increase language awareness. For each of these suggestions make an outline plan of the activities you will undertake with your classes to achieve the awareness suggested.

1 There are occasions when it is useful for teachers and pupils to use grammatical nomenclature (e.g. when you ask, 'How do the adjectives in this poem help create a sombre mood?'). So, early in secondary school, we might distinguish the *functions* of noun, verb, adjective, adverb, conjunction, pronoun, preposition, subject, predicate. *These should arise as an adjunct to looking at the way we use language for particular effects.*

Choose one of these terms and relate it to some ongoing writing and reading with one of your classes (e.g. adjectives in relation to a piece of descriptive writing).

2 There is often an assumption that there is a 'correct' way of handling language applicable to *all* language contexts. You can discuss what 'correctness' means with your classes. Try to do this in a spirit of enquiry. Plan a lesson with a fourth year class to show that 'correctness' is usually a matter of social convention, of 'appropriateness' for a particular situation. You could begin by carrying out a survey, using a dozen disputed 'rules', of the views of other pupils, parents and teachers.

3 It is useful to discuss the differences of convention between written and spoken language. Plan a lesson in which pairs of pupils (a) tape an explanation by one to the other of an incident, picture, game, etc., (b) write an explanation of the same. An ensuing discussion about the differences should bring out some useful points.

4 Accent and dialect are important matters to discuss with your pupils and will raise all kinds of issues about attitudes to language. Don Smedley describes a simple starting point in *Teaching the Basic Skills* (Methuen, 1983, p. 152) for a third-year class: the teacher pre-records a passage read in seven different accents ('upper class', RP, 'educated' local, broad local, Glaswegian, Geordie, West Country). Pupils see if they can guess anything about the speakers (where they're from, what kind of jobs they do, education, type of house they live in, etc.) In small groups they share their impressions and the class as a whole discuss what they think. The teacher then reveals that five accents were by someone imitating that kind of accent. This leads to a discussion of why some accents are generally held to be preferable to others and the resulting stereotyping and prejudice.

REMEMBER What these and similar exercises are intended to do is to encourage children to examine the rich diversity of everyday language uses 'so that they become the masters of language and not its victims.' (Smedley, 1983)

Follow-up

1 Try out with your classes some of the other practical tasks suggested in D. Smedley, *Teaching the Basic Skills* (Methuen, 1983).
2 If you want your pupils to undertake studies in the area of correctness and usage you might find W.H. Mittins, *Attitudes to English Usage* (Oxford, 1970) useful as a resource for the necessary background knowledge you yourself need. P. Doughty et al., *Language in Use* (Arnold, 1971) is a very practical set of 100 lesson topics on all aspects of language and its social context.

**Topic D
CREATIVE WRITING**

Some years ago creative writing figured very prominently in the work of English teachers who considered themselves to be in the forefront of their subject. It was part of a reaction to what was thought to be the sterile rigidity of a diet of grammar, essays and literary appreciation that allowed no room for the personal expression of feelings and for the individual to communicate his or her own sense of what it felt like to be human. The creative writing movement emphasised the importance of pupils being asked to write about themselves from their innermost resources (feelings, memories, experiences), 'creating' a highly personal piece of writing rather than imitating established public models.

The pupils' writing was to be accepted as having an integrity of its own and they were encouraged to produce in their own way what they could do best. The finished product was assessed for liveliness and imagination more than for correctness of the basic skills. It was what was thought by some to be an undue emphasis on self-expression at the expense of handling basic skills that tended to bring creative writing into disrepute.

Nowadays, perhaps, a more balanced approach holds sway. Creative writing is one, albeit a vital one, of the many kinds of writing encouraged in the best English classrooms. It is regarded as important for the way in which it contributes to the individual's personal growth and, most often, is defined as any personal writing expressing the individual's experiences and exploring and expressing inner feelings in a language that vividly and vitally *recreates* what it feels like to be in a certain state, situation or mood.

Most of what was said about setting, structuring and responding to writing in Part 2 is relevant to creative writing tasks. Activity 18 adds some particular points associated with personal writing. It is useful to begin with a brief example of a creative writing task set up in one teacher's third-year class:

Over two lessons the teacher led them into talking about how they felt about the area they lived in. It was their personal feelings that mattered – no matter what prejudices or exaggerations might be expressed. They had looked at, and talked about photographs of many different streets; read and discussed some of Douglas Dunn's poems from *Terry Street* and a prose description of life on a housing estate written by a 13-year-old girl. They talked as a class and in small groups, compiling lists of thoughts, associations, memories and feelings about 'life down our street' and looked via the Dunn poems at ways of creating images that expressed their emotional reactions to places. Finally they were asked to write in poetry or prose about where they lived under the title 'Look What I See'. They were asked to recreate the atmosphere of the place, bringing the scene alive through a vivid description of their street and their reactions to life in it.

Activity 18: Planning a creative writing task

Plan a lesson(s) leading to writing of a personal kind that expresses the writer's genuine feelings, and which is designed to help them to honestly explore their personal perceptions of something. In planning remember what was said in Part 2 about structuring a writing task. Then complete the planning and organisation steps below.

Planning stages	*Action to be taken in the lesson*
1 What will be your opener and what will you focus on? (direct experience, anecdote, poem, film, etc.?)	
2 Will you use talk (possibly in groups/pairs) for collecting, relating, jotting, formulating ideas? How?	
3 (a) When/how will task be defined? (will you involve pupils in this?) (b) Decide priorities in their approach to the writing.	
4 (a) Writing in drafts: first draft discussed with partner. Encourage changes. Share examples with class. (b) Help reluctant with suggestions.	
5 Revised draft(s): swap with others, extend ideas, enliven language, produce final copy.	
6 Share finished copy (read aloud, duplicate, display) and discuss results in class.	

These steps are adapted from R. Protherough, *Encouraging Writing* (Methuen, 1983, pp. 58-59, 182-183.)

Follow-up

1 At the earliest opportunity teach the lesson you've planned. Afterwards evaluate the lesson, asking yourself these questions:
 ... is there evidence that your pupils grasp that this kind of writing requires word-energy, liveliness of expression, etc.?
 ... have your pupils really closed in on the subject, being prepared to honestly explore their personal feelings?
 ... what kinds of things do you think you should spend more time on if you are to increase pupils' awareness of writing as a creative craft?

We are not in the business of producing little Shakespeares. It is not complete originality that we seek. Encourage pupils to break what is new ground *for them* in the battle to put experience into words. That will be true creativity and originality.

**Topic E
FICTION FOR
TEENAGERS: WHAT
IS AVAILABLE?**

Promoting pupils' enjoyment of reading fiction is partly a matter of being able to help them find the right book at the right time. To be in a position to do this you need to have given some thought to what kinds of books are available. Activity 19 will help you to do this, and Activity 20 should give you some help with those readers reluctant to actually get to grips with books. Before undertaking these activities it is important to remind yourself that if you are to interest your pupils in reading, some preliminary essentials have to be observed.

These are essentials for creating a pleasurable reading climate:
... To be informed, you should be a regular reader of books for children, keeping abreast of some of the better known authors' work.
... There should be books of all kinds available in the classroom and these should constantly be referred to or read in lessons.
... There should be regular times for silent reading for pleasure (you yourself should be seen reading at some of these times) as well as times when you introduce and talk about books you think your pupils would enjoy.
... Links should be made between TV programmes and reading.

**Activity 19:
Deciding on criteria
for fiction**

There follows a list of possible criteria to which the books you use and recommend to children might conform. Try to place them in order of priority having regard to the ages and ability of the particular group of children you have in mind.

Criteria	*Priority*	*Comment on age and ability*
A narrative that is clear, exciting and interesting with moving incidents		
Characters that go beyond stereotypes with their conflicts and relationships bearing much of the story's meaning		
Story with some humour and/or suspense and a plot with a good pace		
Narrative that presents life through eyes of young people (although not necessarily young narrator)		

Any other criteria you consider important?

How do you apply such criteria? The titles of four books popular with many English teachers are given below. Try to read three of these, and persuade some of your pupils to do so as well. Then organise an informal discussion to find out what they thought was attractive about the books or what they didn't like. This should give you some guidance as to what factors to consider in the future when you are making choices of books to give to pupils.

1. Peter Dickinson, *The Devil's Children* (Puffin). Fast-moving adventure raising interesting questions about the future, about life without machinery and about the Sikh religion and culture.
(3rd year)

2. Robert Leeson, *The Third Class Genie* (Fontana Lions). Action packed adventure with well-developed characters. Plot raises questions about wishes, triumphs, disasters.
(2nd year)

3. Gene Kemp, *The Turbulent Term of Tyke Tyler* (Puffin). Short, easy to read, full of action. Centres on adventures and troubles at school.
(1st year)

4. Paul Zindel, *The Pigman* (Macmillan Topliner). American story about relationship between two teenagers and lonely old man resulting in tragedy. Thoughts about youthful high spirits and consequences of thoughtlessness.
(4th year)

It is important, but difficult, to match the right book with the right child at the right moment. Yet this is essential if we are to encourage voluntary reading for pleasure. Recommending books for pupils requires the teacher to know something about the individual child's interests, which is one reason why he should take every opportunity to talk informally to as many pupils as possible. It also demands that we ourselves read as many books as possible and that we know what is being published. One way of keeping abreast of new fiction is to scan the reviews that appear in the following periodicals:

The English Magazine
Use of English
Signal
The School Library Association Journal
Times Educational Supplement

The reluctant reader

Not all pupils read books. If we believe in the importance of voluntary reading we must try and do something for the reluctant readers. A reluctant reader is not someone who lacks reading ability but someone who can read but chooses not to do so. To encourage such pupils to read we need (a) to learn something of their interests, and (b) to be aware of books published especially for those who require simple (but not childish) texts. Activity 20 suggests ways of building up a profile of readers' interests and ways of encouraging them to read.

Activity 20: Encouraging the reluctant reader

Complete the profile document given below. Do this over a period of time: eight weeks or a term. Then carry out the suggestions in the Follow-up Section.

Suggested task	Which class/group will you try this with? How will you organise it?
1 *Reading inventory* Get an idea of what pupils like to read, what excites them and what they find boring, by constructing a questionnaire that they can answer every time they read a book, magazine, comic, etc. Carry this out over two months. To avoid it becoming boring have the occasional session in which pupils tell each other about their answers; or have them tape instead of write a report. Use results to build a profile of interests. Possible questions include: – did you like the beginning of this book? What caught your attention? – which comics, and magazines do you like? – do you like stories about people like yourself or people/places very different from what you know? – what TV programmes do you like? **2 *Reading interviews*** You can use the above inventory as an input for this. Select three or four pupils to talk to informally, but in detail, about their reading habits. Look at some books with them. Carry out the interview in a pleasant, encouraging manner, trying not to be moralistic about reading. **3 *Prediction task*** Give small groups (six or eight) a story or extract to read together in instalments. Between instalments get them to discuss what they think will happen next and *why* (this is essential). Predicting the outcome increases commitment to reading and the reasoning involves the questioning of the text – a step towards becoming an active reader.	

Follow-up

Very useful commentaries on how to develop pupils' response to reading fiction, together with reliable lists of books enjoyed by adolescents include the following. Read at least one and try to adapt some of the classroom suggestions to your own teaching:

David Jackson, *Continuity in Secondary English* (Methuen, 1983)

Robert Protherough, *Developing Response to Fiction* (Open University, 1983)

And two books concerned with reluctant readers:

J. Foster (ed.), *Reluctant to Read?* (Ward Lock Educational, 1977)

Reading After Ten (BBC Publications)

Topic F
THE MASS MEDIA

The mass media dominate the means by which our society expresses itself. We are not an exclusively literary society and English teachers who see the subject as being concerned with *all* the modes of language argue that some study of the media should be a part of English. There has been a divided response to such calls for media and communications studies. While some argue that their training in literary discrimination gives them skills to help pupils to analyse the forms of the media, others passionately condemn the trivialising values of the media and reject any idea that they are a fit object of study. But surely such views serve only to reinforce pupils' views that their world is alien to schools and teachers. Researchers have found that many pupils gravitate towards the world offered by television, pop radio, and teenage magazines precisely because it offers them patterns of meaning and expression denied them within school. It would seem better to seek to help them understand the nature of the world offered by the media.

What might be done by English teachers? There are two basic approaches which could be incorporated into the present curriculum without jettisoning any of the other things done: (a) to explore pupils' responses to the form and content of the media, (b) to develop an awareness of how the media work sufficient to help pupils to recognise the ways in which the media manipulate responses.

(a) exploring responses to media (all ages/abilities)	Things that pupils read, watch, listen to, should be part of resources for our activities in English. What pupils are interested in, moved by, irritated by, etc. should provide starting points for exploring topics raised by their responses to the media. The media are part of our shared experience and we should welcome it as a talking point and launching pad for ideas for lessons.
(b) understanding how the media work (14-18)	We can help pupils become more aware of the variety of intentions, formats and effects of TV programmes, newspapers and magazines, pop music, advertising, etc. We can try to show them how these media fit into society, how they are created (e.g. how camera angles, editing, etc. contribute to a programme's effect) and by making them aware of this give them the means to critically assess the social/ personal effects of the media.

Activity 21:
Looking into the media

There are two parts to this activity. In the first you are given examples of two classroom tasks that one teacher had his pupils undertake in a series of lessons called *The Persuaders*. In the second part you are asked to plan and teach some lessons of your own which are intended to raise your pupils' awareness of the nature of the media.

Part 1 The Persuaders

A teacher and his fourth-year class were looking at the ways in which advertising, the newspapers, and some kinds of TV programmes try to buttonhole the reader/viewer and get him to accept what they say as the truth or to do something they want (e.g. purchase particular goods). The link between these lessons was *the ways in which words and images are used to persuade*. As far as possible, the teacher wanted his class to discover for themselves how language was being manipulated for particular ends, so he devised a series of tasks for pupils to do in small groups. Some were basically 'thinking' tasks and some 'doing' tasks. Here are two examples. Write in the right hand column what you suppose the aim of each task to be — what might we expect the pupils to learn from undertaking such tasks?

Task	What aims?
To do: (a) select six adverts from TV, papers or magazines and compare the kinds of *information* they give on their products. *What* are we told? What *not* told? (b) Try to buy one or two of these products. By using them can you say if the adverts are accurate/distorted, the facts selected, etc.? (c) Use your evidence to write a brief explanation of *how* information is handled and try to form a judgement as to the *purpose* of the advertising (there's more to it than *just* selling the product — think of how they appeal to the buyer)	
To think: TV commercials constantly make use of the same types of characters again and again (stereotypes such as the harassed, headachy secretary, or housewife who doesn't know about a famous labour-saving gadget, or north-country farmer with honest accent and no-nonsense voice). Watch a few evenings' commercials and list as many stereotypes as you can find; describe the context in which they occur and decide what each is used for by the advertiser. Why do you think such stock characters are used?	

Part 2 Understanding your intentions

You are now going to consider what you might do to help your pupils be more aware of the intentions, formats, and effects of the media. Below are three suggested aims for parts of different themes concerned with aspects of the media (age levels of pupils who could undertake these aims are indicated). Your task is to outline a way of achieving each aim. Remember the doing and thinking activities from Part 1.

Suggested aim (Helping pupils to understand that . . .)	*Possible tasks for pupils*
1 In newspapers, magazines and on TV, adverts use words and pictures to *persuade* the consumer to purchase far more than they do to *describe* their products. (3rd year?)	
2 Newspapers assume different styles of presentation for different kinds of readers (both in handling news as well as features like sport, fashion, entertainment, gossip, etc.) (4th year?)	
3 TV documentary and news programmes select and edit their pictures and commentaries. The way they are organised and structured always implies some point of view even when they would have us believe they are neutral. (4th-6th years?)	

Follow-up

1 Try to include at least one of the tasks from Part 2 in your future teaching and at the end of it ask your pupils what they think they have learnt from the tasks, and try to discover what aspects of media study they would find most interesting.

2 There are now quite a lot of textbooks that help with media study, but the following are most easily available and contain suggestions for classroom activities:

R.B. Heath, *The Persuaders* (Nelson, 1975) and other titles in the same series;

Making a Newspaper available from The English Centre, Sutherland St, London SW1;

L. Masterman, *Teaching About Television* (Macmillan, 1980) is invaluable;

for a general review see G. Murdoch and I. Phelps, *Mass Media and the Secondary School* (Macmillan, 1973).

SELECTED READING

The following books are all chosen because they contain discussions and/or examples of activities you could try out in your classrooms.

Continuity in Secondary English, David Jackson (Methuen, 1983)
Teaching English, Tricia Evans (Croom Helm, 1981)
Every English Teacher, A. Adams and J. Pearce (Oxford, 1974)
Encouraging Writing, Robert Protherough (Methuen, 1983)
Patterns of Language, L. Stratta, J. Dixon, and A. Wilkinson (Heinemann, 1973)
Encounters with Books: Fiction 11-16, David Jackson (Methuen, 1983)
Developing Response to Fiction, Robert Protherough (Open University, 1983)
Does it Have to Rhyme? Sandy Brownjohn (Hodder & Stoughton, 1982)
Poetry Experience, Stephen Tunnicliffe (Methuen, 1984)
Marking & Assessment, Pauline Chater (Methuen, 1984)
Mark My Words, T. Dunsbee and T. Ford (Ward Lock Educational, 1980)
Encouraging Talk, Lewis Knowles (Methuen, 1983)
Teaching the Basic Skills, Don Smedley (Methuen, 1983)
Growth Through English, John Dixon (Oxford, rev. ed. 1975)
Teaching English Across the Ability Range, R.W. Mills (Ward Lock, 1977)
Thinking About English, M. Paffard (Ward Lock Educational, 1979)
Assessing Children's Language, A. Stibbs (Ward Lock Educational, 1979)
English Teaching Since 1965, David Allen (Heinemann Educational, 1979)
Working with Fiction, Mike Hayhoe and Stephen Parker (Arnold, 1984)
Report of the Bullock Committee on Teaching English, *Language for Life* (HMSO, 1975)

An English teacher is the master of the first word, not the last word.